I0080188

BOYS

WILL BE

MEN

A GUY'S
GUIDE TO
FATHERHOOD

CHRISTOPHER J. WEEKS

Copyright © 2021 Christopher J. Weeks

Published by Doorway Publishing

All rights reserved. No part of this publication may be reproduced or transmitted in any form or by any means electronic or mechanical, including photocopy, recording, or any information storage and retrieval system now known or to be invented, without permission in writing from the publisher, except by a reviewer who wishes to quote brief passages for inclusion in a magazine, newspaper, website, book or broadcast.

ISBN: 978-1-954771-02-4

Published in the United States of America

www.christopherjweeks.com

CONTENTS

Dedicated to my lovely mother,
Rita Mae.

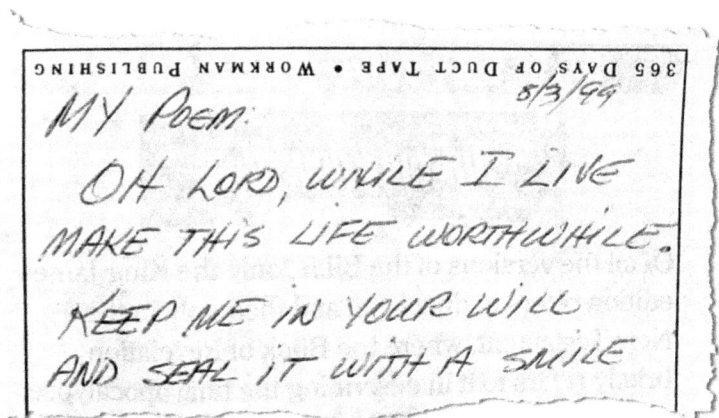

MY POEM:

OH LORD, WHILE I LIVE
MAKE THIS LIFE WORTHWHILE.
KEEP ME IN YOUR WILL
AND SEAL IT WITH A SMILE

8/3/99

365 DAYS OF DUCT TAPE • WORKMAN PUBLISHING

Written by Donald Charles Weeks

PURPOSE:
Why Does a Dad Matter?

How do you know if you're missing something if you never had it in the first place? Well, as the old saying goes, "You'll never know what you're missing." This simple truth is rather obvious for most things in life. A person who has been born blind can never understand the wonder of seeing a summer sunset as it vanishes behind the Pacific horizon on a clear July night. Or a completely deaf person will never be moved by the opening brass fanfare of the Monday Night Football theme song in the same way a ten-year-old football fanatic from Cleveland with perfect hearing will be. And yet, when it comes to the role of dad this truth is simply ignored and tossed aside by many as irrelevant or unimportant. Just try to explain how necessary fathers are in a society that has systematically attacked and degraded them for the last 30 years. Children are no longer taught that when dad is gone from the home, they are missing a truly wonderful thing.

Dads have become expendable. They are the unwanted guest at the dinner party—the mindless ogre that is best left alone grunting and scratching in his man cave down in the bowels of the basement. Having a father in the home is no longer considered to be a basic foundation stone for raising healthy children. And because of this lack of urgency about the importance of dads, an untold number of people "will never know what they're missing." Even worse, some people have had such a bad dad growing up that even hinting at the notion of having a male figure as the head of the home sounds like you want people condemned to a life of misery. Bad dads have brought untold harm on their children, leaving scars and emotional wounds that will be passed on for countless generations. And therefore, this has caused a societal backlash on all dads.

Because of this backlash, some in the church believe there must be some sort of grand-scale conspiracy to rid the home of all fathers. In some conservative circles there is a secret fear that a vast militant feminist movement exists behind the scenes hellbent on eliminating and expunging all dads from the world. Behind every news story and television sitcom they imagine some nefarious plan to destroy the male sex.

Perhaps there is a vocal anti-male sentiment in our country, but I don't think people want to do away with the role of father as much as it appears. I am more inclined to believe that good dads just don't get good press as they should because they are so busy keeping the world afloat, they don't have time to demand attention or argue their importance. Good dads never lower themselves to play the victim, nor do they need to be noticed. They silently keep on keeping on.

In my opinion, what good dads need is an advocate, someone to make their case for them and help explain why they matter. Instead of getting angry and spending all our time arguing against the massive cultural experiments—such as transgenderism, gender fluidity, and homosexual confusion—I think it would be more constructive to promote society's desperate need for good dads.

Dads matter! And to help explain why I want to tell stories about my own dad. The argument to be made in favor of dad is not a competition between the sexes, nor am not pointing any fingers at single mothers, or here to complain against the homosexual's celebration of having two moms. I believe the greatest defense for the importance of having a dad in the home is to help you, the reader who may see no need for dads, get a good look at what you are missing!

In Romans 11:11 Paul says, "Salvation has come to the Gentiles to make Israel jealous." In the same way, I am convinced the greatest argument for a dad is to make men who have never had a good dad wish they had one. And then after jealousy kicks in, they will go to the next step and will long to become one. I am convinced that the current backlash toward men and fathers is stoked by subconscious jealousy born out of wanting something they never had, and because they never had it, they don't want others to enjoy the benefits of it.

The retaliation against dads in popular culture is nothing more than the tragic replaying of "King Solomon and the Baby."

In 1 Kings 3:16-28, two women lived in the same house and both had a young baby. One of the women suffocated her baby in her sleep by rolling over it. When she realized what she did, she switched her dead baby with the other woman's live baby in the middle of the night. The next morning when the real mother tried to nurse her baby, she found that it was dead, but after close inspection, she realized it wasn't her baby, and that they had been switched. Outraged, she brought the case before King Solomon.

King Solomon listened to the facts of the tragic situation and in his wisdom declared, "Cut the living child in two, and give half to one woman and half to the other!" The real mother, who loved her child very much, said, "Oh no, my lord! Give her the child—please do not kill him!" Solomon quickly surmised that this was the baby's mother because the heart of a true mother is life. So he gave the rightful mother the living baby.

The moral is simple: Instead of allowing the rightful mother to have her baby, the childless mother would rather see the baby be cut in half, causing certain death. Why would she do this? Jealousy. She would rather be equal in misery than allowing someone else have more than her. That is the essence of a society that does not value life, or the role of the father. Equality that represses is often more welcomed than allowing the joy of the few who actually reap the benefits of following God's beautiful design for family life. That is why I believe dads are so downgraded these days, "If I can't have a good dad, neither can you!"

But God's truth remains, and his design is life-giving. Dads do and always will matter! In fact, they are vital for the health of the home, church community, and nation. Dads are needed for people to thrive.

But the only way to convince you of this is not to argue with you, rather, I will have to show you. It is like the old grade school game of show-and-tell—in order to understand you must first see. That is what this book is going to attempt. I want to show you up close and personal pictures of a dad who actually lived life to the fullest instead of lecturing about it. He was a man who sacrificed instead of demanded, and who simply loved his wife, his children, and most of all, his God.

To paraphrase Orwell in "1984", "It is not by winning an argument but by keeping yourself grounded in reality that you carry on the human heritage." As I was talking to a friend about the book I was writing, he asked, "What makes you think that your dad is better than any other?" That is the point, I don't. I am just telling you my story. So let's get on with it, let me show you my dad…

INTRODUCTION:
Ride the Bike!

"You fathers—if your children ask for a fish, do you give them a
snake instead? Or if they ask for an egg, do you give them a
scorpion? Of course not! So if you sinful people know how to give
good gifts to your children, how much more will your heavenly
Father give the Holy Spirit to those who ask him."
—*Luke 11:11-13*

Some kids have it bad from birth. They may be born with pesky abnormalities like a big red nose, a lazy eye, or a club foot. Or in my case, I was cursed with a guilt complex a mile long. Not only did I expect only clumps of black coal in my stocking for Christmas, but when bad things happened in life—like if the dog ran away, the family television was damaged by a fire poker, or there was dog poop smeared across the living room carpet—I usually had something to do with it. Even if I didn't do it, I was the first one to apologize. Maybe it is because I was the youngest child and I didn't want to be seen as a pest, or because I was a bit of a klutz, whatever the reason my guilt complex ran so deep that I always expected the worst and rarely hoped for the best.

I would often stand on the railroad tracks that ran behind our house, looking up at the sky expecting dark rain clouds to instantly appear and ruin my plans for the day. Even if it was a bright and sunny Saturday afternoon, I was confident that my scheduled baseball game or trip to Lake Erie with my friends to go swimming would be completely ruined by a surprise tornado or a sighting of Jaws in the shallows of the shoreline which would shut down the beach. You could say I was a neurotic kid. I often felt that the Sunday comic "Born Loser", which was featured in the Cleveland Plain Dealer newspaper when I grew up, was surely written with me in mind.

So with this truth about me disclosed, I must tell you about one early Sunday morning in August that this guilt-ridden neurotic boy will never forget. It was an especially hot and humid day and sweat was causing my cut-off Cleveland Browns pajamas bottoms to stick to my thighs. I was laying down on the bottom bunk in my bedroom, covers pulled off, and I was tossing and turning trying to find some comfort before I had to wake up to get dressed for church. I noticed the door of my room slowly began to crack open and my dad peeked his dark head of hair in and said, "Chris, wake up and come outside with me."

I looked at my electric Panasonic digital flip clock that read 6:47 a.m. It seemed awfully early to get up for a Sunday morning. The Davey and Goliath cartoon, my Sunday morning staple, wasn't on until 8 a.m. I rubbed my eyes with the back of my fisted hand and slowly followed my dad down the stairs and out the back door. He was wearing a pair of dark blue Bermuda shorts and a white t-shirt from the day before. And I am pretty sure he had a used toothpick tucked behind the flap of his right ear.

I noticed that it was unusually bright as I stood on the hot pavement of our driveway. I could feel the heat from the rough concrete warming the bottom of my bare feet as I wondered to myself, *Why is my dad getting me up so early?* He smiled and pointed to the large sliding sectional garage door. Normally the door was opened, but for some reason my dad had it closed.

"Pull her open," he said.

"Why dad? I am so tired and hot," I whined back, expecting him to be upset at me for how poorly I cut the lawn the day before. Or maybe I didn't put the hedge clippers away in the right spot on the pegboard on the garage wall.

"Chris, just open the door and you'll see." He said, rubbing his thick hands together in bubbly anticipation.

I went over to the garage door and bent down to grab the silver metal handle, wondering why my dad seemed so excited. I began to pull up, letting the counterbalance weight do most of the work. I can still hear the sound of the rusty rollers scrape and squeak against the metal overhead door track. At first, I was only looking down at my bare feet thinking how hot they were, but as I slowly lifted my head my eyes began to focus on something unusual that was hiding in our dark musty garage. And then, I saw it!

There in the center of our garage was a brand-new blue Schwinn Stingray pedal bike. It was fully outfitted with a white faux-leather banana seat and long chopper handlebars complete with white grips and red, white, and blue tassels coming off the end. It was the same exact bike I would stare at in the store window of the local Roger's and Wray's general store. I was dumbfounded. Standing before the shiny new bike my mouth hung wide open in shock. I couldn't believe what I was seeing. My dad bought me the bike of my dreams. *How did he know?*

But then a more powerful thought overwhelmed my small guilt-ridden mind, *How could he afford it?* The week before my birthday I was eavesdropping on my mom and dad, listening to them discuss the family's tight finances. It was late at night and I was sitting at the top of the staircase when I overheard my dad explaining to my mom how he had a slow month of sales. And as a result, the whole family needed to tighten their budgetary belts. And now, a week later on this especially bright Sunday morning, here was a brand new expensive-looking bike standing right in front of me.

"Dad," I said, "you didn't have to buy me that bike. It's brand new, and plus, I know we're tight on money."

My dad looked at me with an exasperated tight-lipped look. I knew that look—I said something that was not what he wanted to hear. He took a deep breath and replied, "Chris, don't worry about it. Just get on the darn bike and ride it."

"But dad," I kept on, "I don't deserve it and it really looks expensive."

I could see my dad was losing his patience with my unwarranted self-pity, so he pointed at the bike and said in a much sharper tone, "Chris, I bought this for you as a gift. Get on the bike! Ride the bike!"

Instead of allowing fear, worry, an overactive guilt complex, and self-pity to rob me of joy, my dad knew that I needed his help to allow the love he wanted me to experience. That is what a good dad does, he encourages the timid heart. Under his care, he wanted his children to be free to explore, enjoy, and not be weighed down by things that they should not, and cannot, be responsible for. "Ride the Bike" has become for me an expression of the good dad's desire for his children to "embrace grace"—and grace is not a deserved thing, but it is a gift given out of the Father's undying love for us. And it is this same grace that makes everything possible and life worth living.

This is the true heart of a good dad. He cares more for those under his care than himself. Psalm 112 says the good man is both "generous" and "has no fear of bad news." This was the heart of my dad, and this is what I wish everyone could experience. There is nothing comparable to the love of a good father.

ONE:
Made in Cleveland

"Nazareth! Can anything good come from there?"
— *John 2:46*

My dad was a "Honyak", and I loved him for it. But to many people, especially to a sophisticated, trend-chasing, fashionably current person, "Honyak" has a cringe-worthy, "living in a van down by the river" ring to it—a crude moniker meant only for the dregs of the society. And it is definitely not something you should be praising your father for. The real difficulty with the word Honyak is that trying to define it can be a rather tricky task. If you grew up hearing the word it was often used as a light-hearted term of endearment, or a way to make fun of someone in a playful way, "You Honyak!" To know a Honyak was to love a Honyak. But that doesn't help the reader, who has never heard the word before, understand it. So let me try to explain it for you.

The word *Honyak* has nothing to do with ethnicity, race, or even social standing. But rather it has everything to do with style and substance. If you would look up the definition for *Honyak* you will find a wide variety of descriptions and strange etymologies of the origins of this word. Here are some common understandings of Honyak:

(1) Some people think the word Honyak comes from Central or Eastern European slang used for an uncouth peasant or person who lived a hardpan life.

(2) A Honyak is sometimes used to describe an oafish or sloppy person who has no consideration for cultural norms or accepted standards of behavior.

(3) A Honyak is an urban hillbilly.

But my favorite definition I found in my research is this:

(4) A Honyak is often used in a jocular or affectionate way when addressing one's family or friends for their down-to-earth and unpretentious nature.

If you were to pour all four of those definitions into one large glass and stir, you have my dad. Even though he looked and sang like Elvis, was highly successful in the business world, and was an amazing athlete to boot, inside of the core of his being lied a true Honyak. These character qualities formed him into a person that was not easily swayed by what the world around him was constantly competing for and fighting about: Popularity, prestige, and public success. In fact, when it came to making a name for himself, he could care less. I describe this Honyak character quality as the "Cleveland" in him.

Cleveland, Ohio is a town that is often laughed at. It is the "Nazareth" of America, where people often wonder, "Can anything good come from Cleveland?" Known for its brutally cold winters, rusty cars, and a river that once caught on fire from industrial pollution, Cleveland is certainly not the first-place people think of when they are looking for the "top ten cities to visit on vacation." But I would humbly argue that it is the perfect place to raise a Honyak like my dad.

A HARDPAN LIFE

If you have ever watched "A Christmas Story" and saw the house that the main character Ralphie grew up in, you got a first-hand glimpse of where my dad grew up; minus the stiletto-legged lampshade, of course. The filming of the movie took place in the same poor neighborhood of Cleveland, Ohio where my dad lived as a boy. It was close to downtown Cleveland and it was populated with a variety of poor ethnic families full of working-class people.

My dad's father, my grandfather, worked most of his life as a humble parking lot attendant. Sitting for long hours in his booth he spent most of his married adult years collecting the local businessmen's parking money, day after long day, week after monotonous week. This was not the job a person would boast about or see as the ultimate goal on his quest to achieve his highest human potential in life. A parking lot attendant is not the dream job that the motivational speaker and prosperity preachers would point to as reaching the summit on Maslow's hierarchy pyramid. Oh no, it is a humble blue-collar, low-skilled job. But that didn't bother my grandfather, because, like most people of his day, he simply needed to find a consistent well-paying job so he could support his wife and two children. That was enough, he was content. Being able to provide adequate food and shelter for his family was considered a luxury back in his day because all he knew before that was living in a dirt-poor cabin along the shore of Mobile Bay, Alabama. Cleveland was a huge upgrade for him.

My dad's neighborhood was a melting pot of Roman Catholic Italian, Polish, and African American families. Most of the families living there had fathers working long shifts in the grimy steel mills while most mothers were busy at home raising a large brood of kids. Roman Catholics considered birth control a mortal sin back in that day, so my dad said there always seemed to be an abundance of friends you could run around the neighborhood with. In fact, he has nothing but fond memories of his childhood: Playing countless hours of sand-lot baseball with his friends during the hot summer days and stickball in the busy streets right after he finished all of his dinner. He would talk about how he had to share a bedroom with his older sister because the house he was raised in was a little two-bedroom economy house, with a small living room, and kitchen in the back that contained an old oak table that just barely seated a family of four.

Instead of focusing on his family's lack of money, or cry about having only two outfits of clothes to choose from -play clothes from Monday to Saturday and his scratchy Sunday church outfit – he instead told us the stories that brought him laughter. He would remark that joy was abundant in his simple little home and it was fun living in such a close-knit urban community. There was always something to do.

His favorite memories concerned the events surrounding simple everyday family life. He said you didn't have to travel far or spend a lot of money to discover the pleasures of life, because he said it was in knowing people that true joy came. I can remember the joyful tears that would swell up in his eyes as he would describe his dad coming home from work carrying a round ripe watermelon he bought at the local corner market. He would cut the giant green fruit on the top of the steps of the small front porch handing large juicy pieces to my dad and his sister as he encouraged them to take large messy bites. "Don't let your mom know I bought this for you," he would whisper with a mischievous grin. And while they would spit the black seeds at each other his dad would continue to smirk as he sat down on the porch swing whittling away at a stick he found in the back yard.

Many of his poor friends and other neighborhood kids would come over as well and ask for a piece of the melon as they would start up a conversation with his dad watching him as he slowly sliced off a curling layer of bark from the stick with his huge, calloused hands. They all loved listening to his stories of fishing in Mobile Bay as a kid. My dad remembers that the stories he told were always warm and easy because no one ever seemed to be in a hurry when they talked to his dad. Time ran slow and sweet as his kind southern drawl spun fascinating tales of the sleepy Alabama south. It was as if the world stopped as all the kids sat on the stairs and listened spell-bound letting their thoughts be carried away. My dad could imagine himself clear as day sitting on an old two oared fishing skiff that was gently bobbing in the bay on a bright afternoon while his dad was casting nets on the nearby shore snatching up scores of speckled trout and fresh shrimp.

In the evenings his mom would often play John Phillips Sousa marches on an antique upright piano while he and his sister marched around the kitchen table like two tin soldiers. But the highlight of the week was when his Uncle Oscar came over to visit on a Friday or Saturday night. He said, "Then we would have some real fun." His dad would push all of the furniture against the wall, his uncle and dad would take off their shoes, and strip down to their white t-shirt and work pants, and then they would wrestle for hours on the large living room carpet spread out across the hardwood floor while his mom would shake her head and go into the kitchen to cook. "When will you boys ever grow up?" she would say with a look of feigned disgust.

"We didn't have much," my dad would say, "but boy would we laugh."

Cleveland afforded simple pleasures and ample time for long, deep conversations. That is what mattered most to my father. He longed for those easy days more than he did for the days of trying to buy the newest and nicest car, or a big house, and a stocked closet of fine clothes. The humble tastes of a Honyak are rare to find in a person, but when someone has them, they are the happiest people you will ever find because it doesn't take much to keep them satisfied. Growing up in Cleveland formed in him an appreciation for working hard, enjoying people, and finding joy in the small things. He never lost that sweet, simple longing and for his six kids, it was something that was easily caught without having to be taught.

NOT EASILY IMPRESSED

Growing up in the inner-city of Cleveland also forced him to learn about the idiosyncrasies and graces of other ethnic groups firsthand. Because the small houses full of large families were squeezed tightly together on his busy block, he found countless friends everywhere he went. You had no other choice but to learn to respect other people's differences. When different cultures are required to live together in peace, he said you begin to realize that people are people no matter what race, creed, or color they may be. "We all have warts," he would say, "we all have sorrows, and above all, everyone needs God." His favorite phrase that he constantly taught us so we would learn to see others without judgmental scorn and also without patronizing them with false praise was this familiar bromide of his: "There ain't a horse that can't be rode, and there ain't a man who can't be thrown." He insisted that before you judge people, learn people. Because as you learn you will soon see that in general terms, no one's culture is better or worse than any other, regardless of race, salary, or which street they grew up on.

His first memory of learning about different cultures was when he was seven years old playing hide-n-go-seek with his Italian neighbors. What he remembers most is that no one ever wanted to be the first one caught because that person had to be the "chaser" for the next round. In hide-n-go-seek, a chaser had to count to ten with his eyes closed while everyone else hid behind trees and old tires around the back yard, and then once he reached ten, he could chase the other kids who were hiding trying to tag them. But the problem with being a chaser is that at his Italian friend's house, the Grandma was always in charge of the games so no one would cheat. Italians tended to argue, and Grandma and her broom was a sure way to stop all hot tempers.

So while you were counting you had to close your eyes and then bury your head in her white kitchen apron that she wore all day, so you would be sure not to be cheating. My dad would crinkle his nose as he would describe the memory of the apron's pungent smell of stale garlic, "It curled your nose-hairs." He was not sure if it ever got washed. Playing hide-and-go-seek is also the time when he first learned that he could run really fast. "Your choice was simple," he would say, "either you would run away fast so you could be one of the last kids caught or get caught so you were the next victim to count with your nose buried in the old Grandma's garlic apron."

One day my dad said he was no longer allowed to play at his neighbor's house. He asked his friend why, and he said, "Grandma thinks you have the 'Maloik'! The evil eye, so she doesn't want you coming around our house anymore. You bring bad luck." Even though he was confused and felt a bit excluded, he was also relieved to not have to play hide-n-go-seek anymore. That is when he first learned that everyone has their own set of strange superstitions, wacky traditions, and even harbor unfair prejudices, but you need to get over slights fast because those strange people are still your neighbors. If you want to live in peace you need to know when to not take offense and how to take the small faults of the human condition with a grain of salt.

No one is better, no one is worse. Just different. We are all only human.

URBAN HILLBILLY

When you don't have much, you learn to make do with what you have. And when you can't have what you want, don't pout about it but use your imagination to enjoy life in the moment.

If I heard it once, I heard it a thousand times, "Chris, don't complain, at least you have boots to wear in the winter. My frugal mom made me tape a plastic bag over my shoes and use them for boots."

Or this,

"Chris, don't whine about what we are having for dinner. Growing up we never heard of Oscar Meyer Wieners, instead, my mom would slice us pieces of liverwurst and olive loaf my dad brought home from the West Side Market and we would make sandwiches for lunch and dinner. They stunk like rotten fish. So we would plug our nose and take a bite, but hey, we had full bellies!"

With my dad, I also learned to relish the simple things in life. Like the taste of juicy watermelon on a hot day, a warm scrambled eggs breakfast, freshly squeezed lemonade, and hamburgers fried on the grill. He would teach us to savor the taste, and after loading his burger with a fresh layer of ketchup, he would say smiling, "It just doesn't get any better than this!" Have you ever fried hamburger buns in the hamburger grease, then spread some butter, mayonnaise and sprinkle some spicy black pepper on both ends of the bun, layer some sliced red tomatoes that you grew in the garden, stack a few butter pickles and then melt cheese over the burger on the grill? That is what my dad lived for on a Saturday afternoon.

One thing he always tried to do at home was to create experiences for us that were just as good or if not better than paying for the real thing. Take for instance enjoying the luxury of sweating in a sauna to get rid of the toxins from your body. The normal way this happens is a group of men who have memberships at a swanky country club or are traveling on a business trip and they reserved a room at an expensive hotel, there will be a steam room available for guests. These fancy sweat rooms are usually constructed from high-quality poplar or cedar wood used for walls and benches, and hot coals are heating in the middle of the room so you can pour Eucalyptus water over them to create steam that will open the pores of your skin. As the heat rises three or four rich fat men with white cotton towels wrapped around their big bellies will sit and sweat talking about their financial portfolios or how they recently shaved a few points off their golf handicap. My dad went a few times when he was on his business trips and it gave him a great idea, he would create his own sauna at home.

His experiment always took place in the heat of a sweltering summer afternoon. "Chris," he said, "after you are done cutting the grass join me up in the garage attic." I had no idea what he was talking about, but as an obedient son I always said, "Okay dad." Cutting the front and back yards of our house took no more than an hour, I would usually have a pair of short nylon shorts on, no shirt, and my faithful blue Niki tennis shoes, no socks. After I was finished I would push the lawn-mower back into the garage, and my dad would already be up in the attic. "Chris, come on up, it's great in here!" I would climb the thin rickety pull-down, spring-loaded attic stairs and when I got to the small opening there would be my dad sweating like a stuck pig. The heat up in the unventilated room was unbearable.

"Oh, this is the life!" He would say as his face was bent down as a salty stream of sweat trickled off the end of his nose. "Grab a seat on one of the ceiling joists, just don't step on top of the drywall, you might fall through the ceiling." I looked around for a place to sit and I found a thick piece of 2 x 10 sticking up between two rows of pink fiberglass insulation. "Don't touch that pink stuff either, it's really itchy." So there we sat in the thick heat of the attic, while beads of sweat rolled off our skin. "This is like being at Avon Oaks Country Club, and you don't even need to buy a year membership card." He began to belly laugh at the stupidity of it all and watching him laugh made me laugh, and it was always the hottest and longest laughing I can ever remember. I think I sweated off ten pounds just from laughing up there. My mom would hear us and come into the garage wondering, "Where are you two fools?"

"Up here!" My dad would cry.

"Where, in the attic? Don, you are crazy. I am not coming up there, you both are a pair of Honyaks!" See, there it is, Honyaks. We truly were urban hillbillies jerry-rigging our own sauna in the attic.

UNPRETENTIOUS AFFECTION

Being raised by a Honyak is a gift. Because with a Honyak you always know what you have: no lies, no hypocrisy, and no games. My dad would be the first one to admit his flaws, sure his anger often raged, but so did his humility. He was quick to apologize and generous with his praise. Since he had no need to prove himself, he was secure in himself. And a secure person doesn't need to compete.

Cleveland may be an uncouth city that people laugh at, but most Clevelanders I know laughed at themselves first, so they always were able to take laughter from others. Look at the Cleveland Brown's uniforms, pumpkin helmets over topsoil brown jerseys, nothing flashy about that, but we still love them.

The modern American tragedy is that we live in a country where people no longer know how to laugh at themselves. Comedy has become about destroying our enemies, it is a cruel sick kind of laughter. Gone are the Jerry Lewis' and Jack Benny's who could laugh at themselves and ask us to laugh along. Cleveland had Big Chuck and Little John to entertain us on late-night television precisely because they knew Cleveland people were funny, "certain ethnic" humor was their expertise. But this is no longer the case, each personal slight or criticism is like an arrow piercing the soul. Microaggressions are now reasons to go to court. Calling a person by the wrong pronoun can get a professor at a university fired. If a man looks at a pretty woman a bit longer than they should it is decried as more proof that the rape culture in America is alive and well. We are the eggshell generation.

Scripture says, "A wise man looks past insults." Honyaks know how to do this, that is why they laugh, and that is why they live free. No victims here. That is also why a true Honyak is easy to love, when they come into a room they never make things about themselves, instead, they want to get to know you. That was my dad, and I pray a little bit of Honyak resides in me.

TWO:
Great Exploits, Mighty Men, & Infragility

"Benaiah son of Johoiada, a valiant fighter from Kabzeel, performed great exploits. He struck down Moab's two mightiest warriors. He also went down into a pit on a snowy day and killed a lion."
— 2 Samuel 23:20

I am writing this chapter in the midst of still trying to navigate through the debris and flotsam of 2020. It has been a terrible, horrible, no good, very bad year! Riots in the streets, 24/7 political division, social media outrage, false news, cable news, podcast news, and noise, noise, noise, noise, noise everywhere. But the dark shadow that still looms large from this past year is the emergence of a big rampaging monster that continues to devour everything in its path, like Godzilla feasting on poor tiny Tokyo. The monster is the invisible microscopic virus known as Covid-19.

For the last nine months, Covid-19 has virtually shut down the world. Small businesses have been forced to close their doors. Friends and family were told to cancel Thanksgiving and Christmas. Masks are now mandatory. But for me, the most difficult side-effect of Covid-19 was the cancellation of the sports season for my college and high school children. My son's sophomore year of college football has nothing left but the shattered visage of empty stadiums and silent, sad Saturday afternoons frowning underneath the golden haze of a fading autumn sun; a lost season, forever quiet and quickly forgotten.

As I saw all team sports slipping away, I tried to do all I could as a concerned parent and pastor to keep the season still an open possibility. My argument was simple; College and High School kids have little to no risk of picking up the virus while playing outside, and if for no other reason they need a healthy divergence in their life at this stress-filled time. Many people pushed back saying, "The cancellation of sports is only for one year. Isn't it better to do our best to contain the virus and keep students safe, rather than to risk one or two lives with the possibility of contracting the deadly disease?" Even online, a few of my friends, who never played team sports, would comment, "Chris, just have your children find a different avenue for exercise and physical release. Tell them to go jogging, hiking, or walking in the backyard. We all need to fight this virus together."

I responded back that my frustration is not simply about them not being able to exercise or have a lack of physical release. This is about missing opportunities and enjoying the life they have been given to live. Life is short and it is not about hiding, but thriving!

A good friend asked me after reading one of my discussions online, "I don't see why it matters so much to you. You normally are so easy going about most things, what is it about the cancellation of sports that riles you up so much?" I thought long and hard about it, and my reason is simple; because I grew up with a man who saw sports as more than a game. Joining a team expands your experiences. It includes more than winning, it is more about taking risks and learning about who you really are. And it was a big part of what made him the man he was. Let me show you.

A SICK BOY

If you were to go to the world-famous Cleveland Clinic and go down to the old archives, there is probably a dusty manila file folder with the name Donald C. Weeks stored away in some old army green filing cabinet. There, my dad says, you will probably find a long list of his doctor visits when he was a young boy. For the first ten years of his life, my dad was one very sick little fella. He was diagnosed with an untold number of allergies, he constantly fought reoccurring asthma attacks, and even around the age of eight, he suffered through a pretty severe bout of pneumonia where he was laid up in bed for a couple of weeks. But the most difficult season of the year for his weak body was in the cool nights and warm dry days of early fall when the milkweed and ragweed would release their pollen and cause him to sneeze and constrict his breathing. He said it felt like a concrete slab was sitting on his chest.

To help with his breathing, his faithful mom, my fire-eating grandmother, would apply a number of her Polish old-country homespun remedies. On the nights when he couldn't sleep because his chest was tight, she would take a bottle of Vicks Vapor Rub, with its potent menthol odor, and massage it all over his chest. If that wouldn't work, she would then make him sit in the shower room for a half an hour while the hot water steamed up the room, hoping to loosen the phlegm in his lungs. Sometimes during the day when he was gasping for air, to get deeper and fuller breaths, he would do headstands and use deep breathing exercises that he read about in some self-help fitness magazines.

Secretly, I think my dad also believed himself to be an aspiring homeopathic healer because his dad, who knew how to live off the land in Alabama, taught him to pick the large green leaves of Burdock weeds that grew in his backyard and then dry them in his room. After a few days they turned into a crispy dark brown texture, and then he would burn them and breathe in the thick swirling green smoke to try and clear his lungs. I am not sure it did anything but he tried to convince his kids it was a miracle cure for asthma.

But a fresh new wind of change started blowing for him at the tender age of ten when he was invited by a group of neighborhood boys to play some sandlot baseball. It was here where his love for sports began. He spent that whole summer, from early morning to late in the evening, dreaming about making it in the big leagues playing for the local Cleveland Indians. All of this started on an old, abandoned patch of dirt in the outskirts of their poor neighborhood. Before he knew it, my dad found himself growing strong and tan in the hot sun, even his asthma was soon clearing up and his lungs felt renewed. Kids from all around would come each day to test their metal, the competition was always stiff and sometimes fights would break out. But my dad said it was the laughter and the camaraderie of meeting all kinds of new friends that kept them coming back.

Looking back on those days, he said that it was at that time that he gained surprising new confidence in himself that he never had before. On the dusty field with other competitive and talented boys his age, he began to see that he had more strength in him than he ever realized sitting at home hoping to get better. When challenged, his heart leapt at the chance to rise to the occasion. He learned that mental confidence and a spirit that wouldn't quit were far more important than having a strong arm and fast legs. When he was knocked down by the larger boys, or was made fun of by a loudmouthed bully, sports taught him that people often will not put their money where their mouth is when you stand up to them. Instead of giving up, a person of strength takes on the challenge.

The sandlot gave my dad a vision of himself that he never had before and he developed a newfound inner-strength that told him he was capable and could overcome. So when school started back up the next fall, he began to join groups that he never tried before. Student council and leadership clubs started to interest him. But he especially loved being part of the football and basketball teams with his friends. He found quick success on the field and this lasted all through his Junior High and High School years where he became a city-wide all-star.

Sports to him was much more than an outlet for exercise, it was a new and exciting world that taught him how to push himself and explore his talents. Instead of sitting around the neighborhood looking for trouble, my dad had new commitments to keep and responsibilities to fulfill. Coaches taught him to take practice and rules seriously. And he found that there was nothing like having loyal teammates and building real friendships united in a common cause.

AN ENORMOUS OPPORTUNITY

All of his young years of commitment and hard work paid off because in his senior year of High School he was offered a full-ride scholarship to play football at a private college in southern Ohio called the University of Dayton. His wildest dreams came true. Who could ever have thought a poor boy from Cleveland would be offered a chance to learn about the world, tuition-free? And it was sports, what some people call silly games or simple exercise, which gave him the chance to become more.

Truth is, all of us love to watch people who excel in their talents. This isn't just true in sports, but it is a fact in every area of life. Some people are great singers, some are spell-binding in drama, others become chess masters, or are skilled craftsmen with tools, and some are incredible at sports. And when they are, we will watch. God made us all with talents, and as Eric Liddell said in the movie *Chariots of Fire*, "When I run, I feel God's pleasure." Young men, especially, have been made to compete.

Dreaming of great exploits is not wrong, nor is it a trivial matter, it is hardwired into them. And as we all know the best stories are the ones that entail the greatest risk. And when victory is achieved it excites the heart. Life is meant to be lived as a grand adventure, full of challenges and calling us all to at least try. If all we do is hide and play it safe, we will simply wither on a vine.

The campus of the University of Dayton fit my dad like a glove. It wasn't just the sports that he grew to love, it was the world that opened up to him through the opportunities that sports gave him. Paging through a scrapbook of memories that my mom kept of those years were newspaper clippings of the person my dad was becoming. Along with the touchdowns he scored, the yards he gained, and the schools he got to travel to and play against such as Miami of Ohio, Cincinnati, Louisville, were scattered tidbits about how he was becoming much more than an athlete. He was known as "the crooner on the team", he and a fellow lineman were highlighted as some of the up-and-coming artists at school, or there was an article about how he and some of his teammates from Cleveland were becoming inspirations to other poor kids from Cleveland.

But more than anything else, I noticed the deep love and enjoyment he had for other people, especially the guys on his team. He learned to rely on them for encouragement and support much as King David did with the mighty men that he fought alongside with. Together they would endure grueling hot summers of two-a-day practices, during the season they would travel all over the Midwest by bus to compete against stiff competition, and all week long they lived together in close quarters of the athletic dorm and eventually a house he shared with five other guys. The best man, two groomsmen, and the person singing during his wedding were all great friends he acquired from being on the football team together. He even named his first dog, Dugan, after one of the huge linemen that blocked for him during games.

Good, healthy relationships for men with other men are next to impossible to find these days. From the scourge that social media has become and the isolation from playing video games alone in a basement, the need for male human interaction has never been more important. Our society has very few outlets left to help young men find their place in this world. Groups like the Boy Scouts, local hunting clubs, and business clubs are mandated to be inclusive. We are told that toxic masculinity is a poison that has been unleashed on society, so most of the kind men have decided to not be a bother and they have quietly gone into hiding. As the song *I Need a Hero* asks,

Where have all the good men gone and where are all the Gods?
Where's the street wise Hercules to fight the rising odds?
Isn't there a white knight upon a fiery steed?
Late at night I toss and I turn and I dream of what I need

They are not wanted anymore. Men have been asked to shut up and take a seat. And that is why I think sports matter more now than ever before. It may be the only avenue left for men to have male friendships without resorting to seedy bars and beer joints or joining street gangs. My dad had the blessing of being surrounded by men of strong character who in turn helped him to become strong himself. Sports was simply the door that opened these opportunities to connect with others up. For the rest of his life, male friendship was an enormous source of life-long joy for him. The stories he told about those days at the University were abundant. Here are a few…

Some of the Roman Catholic churches in the Dayton area would have all you could eat pancake breakfasts on Saturday mornings to raise money for the local church. Being poor college students, he and three of his lineman buddies would go and end up eating so many pancakes that they were no longer allowed to come. One guy, an offensive tackle named Al Weckle, had such a big appetite that he was put on a watch-list which was handed around to other churches so he would not be allowed in.

His friend, Tom Curtain, would encourage my dad to go with him to a local outdoor mall and set up a drawing easel to try and make some extra spending money. Since my dad was an art major, Tom thought it would be a great idea and convinced my dad to give it a shot. But Tom was a bit of a joker, and always up for a practical joke. So Tom borrowed a silk scarf from a female co-ed and told my dad to tie it around his neck and pretend he could only speak Italian. When they got to the mall, Tom would promote my dad as a famous Italian artist who was in town for the weekend and he would paint portraits at bargain prices. My dad said the portraits he painted were terrible, but people loved him because they thought it was some new Italian avant-garde art.

He said these experiences were more about making the most out of sharing the simple pleasures of life with others than it was trying to make a buck or scam the system. "Life back then was different," my dad would say, "people wanted to laugh together without harming others. If you can't enjoy life with others, what is the point?"

A CASE FOR INFRAGILITY

In the book, *The Coddling of the American Mind*, the writer, Greg Lukianoff, bemoans the natural impulse parents have with treating their children as fragile pieces of porcelain. When we are too quick to protect them from life, he believes it is not helping them grow in maturity and excellence. He writes, "Teaching kids that failures, insults, and painful experiences will do lasting damage is harmful in and of itself. Human beings need physical and mental challenges and stressors or we deteriorate." The term for this idea is "Infragility."

Infragility is the opposite of being fragile. Instead of seeing danger as something that is going to destroy you, Greg Lukianoff sees it as an opportunity to grow and be made better. Like a muscle in the body, the more it is worked and stressed, the stronger it gets. Or like calluses on a farmer's hand, it is from constant labor that the thin thickens. Even Paul the Apostle writes about this idea in Romans 5:3-4, "Not only so, but we also glory in our sufferings, because we know that suffering produces perseverance; perseverance, character; and character, hope." As much as people hate and run from adversity, the writers of scripture see it as one of the main tools God uses to grow us. Even James 1:12 is clear on this, "Blessed is the one who perseveres under trial because, having stood the test, that person will receive the crown of life that the Lord has promised to those who love him."

That is what sports were for my father—a public arena of combat that gave him a chance to struggle and face challenges head-on. He learned early in his life that it was through struggle and challenge that a person found his strength. I remember as a young boy when I wanted to quit, or not join a team out of fear of my size, he would look me in the eyes and say, "It's not the size of the dog in the fight, it's the size of the fight in the dog." Boys need to hear that from their dads. And dads are needed now more than ever before to challenge their sons. Moms by nature don't do that, it is the father that sees how pain is gain. My dad loved sports not for sport's sake, but for the opportunities sports afforded.

A final word on sports. I remember my senior year of football as the captain of my team after we won a pretty easy game.

I came home excited, a chest puffed with pride, and I asked my dad how I did. He looked at me and said, "You did okay. Sure, you won, congratulations, but you didn't give it your all. In fact, I think you could have done so much better." I was angry, really angry. I thought my dad would be happier than that, we won after all. The next week we lost a very close game against a powerhouse team. I can remember coming home dejected with bruises all over my body. I walked into the TV room, turned on a show, and slumped down on the couch feeling like a failure. My dad came over and sat down and said, "Chris, I am really proud of you."

"But we lost. And they beat us up pretty bad out there."

He replied, "Who cares about that? I saw in you something I never saw before—you wouldn't quit. Even when they put you on the line across from some huge guys after a few of your guys got hurt, I saw you working your butt off out there. Now that is the heart of a champion! Proud of you." He rubbed my head and walked away.

Wow! It was at that moment that I really felt loved and I understood how he viewed sports. Success to him was not found in trophies, a cheering crowd, or even having write-ups about you in the newspaper. It was all about what was left on the field. Did you give it your all or not? That is what matters. And soon I learned this was the principle he lived by in all of life.

THREE:
When a Man Loves a Woman

"Charm is deceptive, and beauty does not last;
but a woman who fears the Lord will be greatly praised."
— *Proverbs 31:30*

Can you keep a secret? Did you know men and women are wired differently? We think differently. And we approach life differently. You probably have heard it said that "Men are from Mars; Women are from Venus", but I am not quite sure that assessment is entirely accurate. Because I was born a biological male, and from spending much of my life around brutes in their natural habitats of the locker room and fraternity house, I would say that men more likely have come from the planet Mercury. Mercury is a small, rough-cut, stone-hard planet that is terrifically hot from being forged too close to the sun. And women are not from Venus, that relatively calm planet doesn't quite do them justice. Women clearly are from Jupiter, a gorgeous, larger-than-life planet shrouded in thick clouds of swirling mystery and sometimes violent storms. And from the perspective of men, Jupiter also orbits a bit too close to her sister Saturn, the planet that is always wearing a ring.

Like the barren rock of Mercury, men are accustomed to living in the world of hard-edged facts and figures. To go deeper in the realm of feeling and emotion, you need to somehow blast through the hardened stone of their heart. Women, on the other hand, resemble the dancing clouds of Jupiter. They have no trouble diving into the thick layers of human conversations, exploring emotions, and they know how to always keep a man guessing about what is going on in the inside. When it comes to relating to the other, the two planets could not be more different. Sometimes it even feels like their orbits are lightyears away.

Men are visual, they respond immediately to what they see. Like the planet Mercury, most of their emotional and psychological activity is happening right on the surface. It is not too hard to know what they are thinking. And when they like what they see they are quick to respond. And when it comes to Jupiter, they have no defense for her outward beauty and charm. Like all heavenly bodies, the larger the star the more gravitational pull it has on the smaller, more simplistic planet. And in the same way, there is a strange and mysterious power that a beautiful woman wields on the will of a man. Helen of Troy was once said to have a face that launched a thousand ships.

This power is God-given. To drill down into the iron heart of man God uses the sharpest diamond he can find—a noble woman who fears the Lord. Or coming back to the planetary metaphor, she alone can pull his orbit away from the violet, flashing heat of the sun. And when it happens, it is a wonderful thing to behold. As Proverbs 30:18-19 says…

"There are three things that amaze me—
no, four things that I don't understand:
how an eagle glides through the sky,
how a snake slithers on a rock,
how a ship navigates the ocean,
how a man loves a woman!"

This is where the story of my dad continues; he being a true son of Mercury and the mysterious pull of a woman named Rita who completely changed his orbit. This incredible love story is one of the most important events that formed him into the wonderful dad he came to be.

BEER CANS, BATS, AND THE B.M.O.C.

"Boys will be boys" as they say, and when those same boys are large, athletic men who live in the same fraternity house and are heroes of the gridiron on a small University campus, they soon will become a little "too big for their britches." My dad said around his junior year of college that he and his friends on the football team strutted around the university campus like they were the kings of all they surveyed. He enjoyed his new "Big Man on Campus" status, otherwise known as a B.M.O.C. In case you didn't know, a B.M.O.C. is a person who thinks the sun is shining just for him. Some would call a B.M.O.C. cocky, but my dad would say they were just confident in their greatness, as a twinkle would flash in his eye. He summed up the B.M.O.C.'s attitude years later with one of his favorite playful phrases, "It is hard to be humble when you are as great as I am!"

Life was good in those days for the B.M.O.C. Football groupies comprised of precocious co-eds who would follow them around campus, quick to laugh at all of their jokes, inviting them to their parties and get-togethers. He and his roommates would even convince them to clean their house and cook spaghetti dinners for them. There was always a host of giddy girls lined up who were more than happy to help. My mom remembers visiting the football player's house near campus after she and my dad were dating. She says the first time she walked through the door a pungent odor of stale alcohol was hanging thick in the air. That is because she noticed there was a huge tower made of old empty beer cans stacked seven feet high against the living room wall. Because of the smell, a few of the hungry neighborhood bats were drawn to their open window and hung in the shadows of the ceiling's corners. It took their 80-year-old female landlord to clear out the bats because the B.M.O.C.'s were too scared to do it.

Not only was my dad a popular figure on campus, but he also had a good following of football fans off-campus as well. He was known as the golden boy of the gridiron wearing number 44! Kramer's, which was a local bar near the University of Dayton, had a number of older patrons that loved keeping up with the Dayton Flyer's team. One of those fans was my dad's future father-in-law who faithfully opened up the sports section in the local paper to read about my dad's rushing stats. My mom faintly remembers hearing the name Don Weeks at the breakfast table before work, but she had no real interest in football, and definitely would never lower herself to join the league of fawning female football groupies.

My mom was too smart a lady to mess with the arrogance of blockheaded athletes. She was perfectly content to live in the world of books, ideas, and a fear of God. Growing up, one of my mom's favorite memories were of the times she would take the city bus to the local public library and check out some of her favorite authors; Shakespeare, Milton, and Hemingway, to name a few. While some of her friends panted after the popular athletes at school, she wrote copy for the school paper.

When my dad started playing college football at Dayton my mom was finishing up her senior year at local Fairmont High. She was also part of the Majorettes, a baton squad that would perform half-time shows for her high school team. In a strange twist of fate, before she ever met my dad, several ladies from her Majorette squad were asked to fill in for the University of Dayton's majorette squad to perform for a Thanksgiving Day half-time show. Rita traveled on board the band bus and my dad was with his football team to play the University of Chattanooga, in

Tennessee. They had no idea that the other existed. But it was a good year later before they finally met.

PRETTY WOMAN AT THE POOL

Old River Park was the place to be on a hot summer day in Dayton, Ohio back in the late fifties. Built as a recreational area by *National Cash Register* (NCR) *Company*, Old River Park was one of the largest manmade swimming pools in the nation at that time with diving boards and water slides. The park's founder, Edward Deeds, who was Chairman of the Board at NCR, created an area for NCR's employees and their families to come to relax and be refreshed. My mother, who was working for NCR as a secretary at the time, would often go there with her friends to lay out on blankets and enjoy the summer sun. Old River Park was also a popular hangout for the University of Dayton football players as well. To get into the park, the players would wait by the Old River gate and try to convince a pretty NCR employee to bring them in as their guest.

One hot June day in 1959, my dad and three of his friends used their B.M.O.C. charms on a few NCR girls and were granted access into the park. After a few hours of swimming and clowning around on the diving boards with friends, my dad remembers walking out of the pool and seeing a single beautiful face that changed his life forever—Rita Mae Roeckner. He would say that her looks were a mix of Elizabeth Taylor, Audrey Hepburn, and

Sophia Loren all rolled into one. All he knew is that he wanted to meet this gorgeous girl. One of his teammates named Vic Kristopatis was already friends with my mom and introduced my dad to her. Playing up his tall, dark, and handsome charms, my dad confidently sat down next to her and started up a conversation. After several hours he eventually asked my mom to go out on a date with him two weeks later on a Saturday night.

"I'm sorry," my mom replied, "but I have already made plans with friends to go to the Auto Show in Cincinnati that day."

My dad looked at her with astonishment, "You mean you won't break a date to go out with me?"

My mom smiled and calmly said, "No."

But my dad was persistent, like a hungry dog with a bone dangled before him, when he liked someone, he wouldn't give up the pursuit. Right before he got ready to leave, he asked for her phone number to give her a call. True to his word, he called her that very night, and as my mom tells it, "He proceeded to tell me how honored I should be because it was the first time in over a year that he had called a girl on the phone." My mom was amused, but not yet convinced about the handsome B.M.O.C. She knew the football type and wouldn't fall for it. Rita Mae was no man's empty-headed cheerleader. But my dad was smitten. Cupid's arrow hit him squarely in the heart, and Rita Roeckner was not going to get away.

His sincerity had staying power and in no time, they began dating in early July of that year. Four months later, on October 28 to be precise, my dad came over early to my mom's house to take her out on a date. While she was still upstairs getting dressed, my dad was in the kitchen asking her mother and father's permission to marry their daughter. They were more than delighted. When my mom came downstairs, her parents stayed in the kitchen while my dad asked her to sit down. He told her he wanted to say something before they went out. Clueless about his intentions, she sat down on the couch not thinking anything of it. He got down on his knee and said, "I love you, will you marry me?"

My mom says, "I was totally in shock." And then she remembers thinking to herself, "He really loves me!" It took a while to snap out of her shock but then she said, "Yes!" My dad laughed mostly out of relief and said, "For a while there I wasn't sure what you were going to say." Proverbs 30:18-19 is right, it is an amazing thing how a man loves a woman.

THE TAMING OF THE B.M.O.C.

God has given to the woman an incredible amount of power to melt the heart of a man. A bearskin-wearing caveman has been known to don a top hat and tuxedo to woo the pretty lass who lives in the cave across the river. A mountain hillbilly with a long scruffy beard will shave and take a bubble bath to impress the local city girl he saw milling around the feed store. And a beautiful NCR secretary can turn the swagger of a prideful B.M.O.C. into an adoring fiancé. The world would be a much better place if more women of honor would learn to channel their power to tame the savage beast.

Instead, it seems that feminist leaders want women everywhere to celebrate their newfound sexual freedom. If men can do it, women should also be able to enjoy the exploits of unhindered lust as well. When women become like men, they lose the mystery and enchantment they were first created with. Eve was designed to captivate Adam, but sin is causing the allure to fade. The billion-dollar industry of hard-core pornography is now promoted as proof of a clear victory for the fierce new sexual woman. They are told it takes enormous courage to flaunt their sexual prowess, but they have lost so much in the process. Cardi B's hit song from hell, "WAP", is proof positive that many women have sold out to the sexual spirit of the age, losing the luster that only shines through a pure heart.

The sad part of this new woman's movement is that they are playing right into the senseless male brute's vile desires. Stupid men, deceived by the Devil, want women to sell their souls and purity down the river of depravity. Debauchery in the form of one-night-stands and "friends with benefits" is being sold on the backs of brainwashed women. Gone are the days of long-term commitment. Rare is the woman who waits until men prove their worthiness with a promise and a ring. We need to teach little girls the power that can change a man.

Rita Mae had that power. She was cut from a rarer and more spotless diamond, and she sure knew how to tame the beast.

Shortly after my parents had been engaged, my mom and dad had a double date with his friend Bill, who was a basketball star for the University of Dayton, and his female friend named Lois. After attending a UD football game in the afternoon, they decided to stop at Lois' apartment for a short rest before they went to a dance. When they arrived at the apartment, Lois asked the group if anyone wanted a drink. My mom and Bill said they didn't care for anything but Lois, who harbored a secret crush on my dad, asked him to come with her into the kitchen so he could fix himself a drink. After about ten minutes and lots of giggling, my mom was getting a bit perturbed. She walked into the kitchen door to see what was going on and there was Lois, hanging all over him. Immediately she turned around, walked out the door, put her engagement ring on the table, and asked Bill if he could drive her home. Bill complied, while protesting, "Don is not going to like this."

Straight away my dad called my mom that night, but she refused to answer. He kept calling and each time my mom had her mother pick up the phone and tell Don she didn't want to talk. After the third time, my grandmother told my mom, "Sooner or later you are going to have to talk to him." So my mom acquiesced and said my dad sounded timid and apologetic, saying, "I was trying to tell Lois that I was engaged to you, but she wouldn't leave me alone." He told my mom he didn't want to be mean to her, and that right when he was going to leave the kitchen my mom walked in. In his most conciliatory voice, he asked my mom if he could come over so they could talk.

I asked my mom what happened next, and she said, "Of course I couldn't stay mad at him. So he came over, we made up, and the rest is history!" Eventually, they got married, had six kids, and shared 48 married years of true friendship together. The charm of a beautiful woman worked again; Don Weeks was a B.M.O.C. no more!

TILL DEATH

My siblings and I were able to watch firsthand how my mom and dad loved and enjoyed each other over the years. They were very open about their triumphs and struggles. Did they argue? Yes, a lot. Did they disagree? All the time. Did they have difficulties, downtimes, and even periods where they seemed distanced? Absolutely. Life is hard, but they also made a promise to each other, "Till death do us part." I can remember my dad coming home from a long sales trip from across the country and the enormous stress of work weighed heavy on them both, especially when my mom had to stay at home and raise six kids by herself for most of the week. The pattern was the same; my dad would arrive home exhausted, he would then vent, my mom would push back, and they would be angry for a few hours until my dad would ask for forgiveness and apologize.

But one thing was undeniable; through it all, they remained steadfastly in love with each other. Their love wasn't the sappy romantic kind of love where they were tiptoeing through the tulips or sliding down slopes of slippery rainbows, but it was real day-to-day living. They would often get upset, but they would forgive just as quickly. That was the key. Proverbs 19:22 says what a man really needs is "steadfast love" and when he finds it, it is a beautiful thing. Steadfast love is not fickle, it does not let bad feelings ruin it, and it does not demand good times to keep it. It simply remains.

Marriages in today's culture have become battlegrounds where couples hold grudges like land mines and sling insults like arrows. Things go wrong when men refuse to say they are sorry and when women demand perfection. What they both need is a friend who listens and believes in them and a love that "covers a multitude of sins." My parents learned that Christ's love above all keeps no records of wrongs. That is what my mom and dad had, and because he found a partner that stuck close to him during the ups and downs of life, he was able to give himself fully for the sake of his children.

I remember a moment when my mom came walking in the door with tears in her eyes. My dad was in the kitchen cooking dinner and he noticed she looked really down. "What's wrong Rita?" he asked.

"Oh nothing, I'll get over it." My mom replied.

My dad sat down at the table and asked my mom to tell him what happened. My mom went on to explain how an hour before, she was getting into her car and the edge of her door tapped the car next to hers in the parking lot. Storming out of the car that she nudged was a large red-faced man who was hopping angry. He got into my mom's face and started swearing and calling her all kinds of terrible names. He demanded they exchange phone numbers and addresses because he was going to call his insurance and make her pay.

My dad listened to her intently and asked if she left a big mark on his door. She told him it was a tiny smudge, and nothing more, but the names he called her were incredibly disturbing. My dad gave her a long hug, and with a steel look of determination he put on his jacket, picked up the keys off the table, and said, "Give me his address!" After reaching out his hand to take the paper he added, "Don't worry, I'll be back in an hour."

My sister saw my dad leaving the house and went in to talk to my mom, "Where is Dad going? He does not look happy." My mom sat down and replied, "You don't want to know." An hour later, my dad returned as promised, entered the kitchen, took off his coat, and calmly sat down at the table. By this time two of my sisters, my mom, and I were waiting to hear what happened. "Well," my dad said, "let's just say that guy will never bother you again." My sister asked, "Dad, what did you do?"

He started to laugh and said, "Let's just say we had some words. And I told him if he ever talked to my wife like that again we would have to share more than just words next time." My sisters started laughing too and you could see a giant sense of relief flash across my mom's face. As his son, I have seen my dad angry a number of times and with his muscular body from years of playing football he could be quite an imposing figure. At that moment I felt bad for the guy he went to go see, but one thing is for sure, I knew my dad loved my mom and would fight for her. It was a wonderful example for a son to witness.

There are many lessons a father can teach a son. Many skills can be taught like how to use a hammer, throw a football, drive a car, or cook a juicy burger on the grill. But the greatest skill that is quickly becoming a lost art is how to love a woman well. It may be the single greatest lesson I have learned watching my dad. I am also convinced every child would give the world to see their parents in love. Riches, nice cars, and fashionable clothes can never compare to a home where parents are friends. All good dads first love their wives; that is where it must begin.

FOUR:
My Dad's Favorite Hobby

"This is my Son, whom I love; with him I am well pleased."
— Matthew 3:17

Seven minutes! That's it, seven lousy minutes. And what is most surprising is that most people who hear this will not be appalled or outraged at this number. But think about it, seven minutes is nothing. It is how long your average silly YouTube video takes to watch. Or it is about the length of time it takes to cook a small ham and cheese omelet. Or worse, that is all it takes to put on your work boots and Carhartt jacket to go out and check the mail. Only a mere seven, tiny, miserable minutes. And seven minutes also happens to be the average amount of time a dad spends with his kids daily—his very own flesh and blood—each and every day of their growing up years. Seven lousy minutes.

Psychologists, therapists, teachers, and pediatricians alike all say that it is imperative that parents spend time with their children if they want them to grow up into healthy adults. And it is most important to spend that vital time in the first five to seven years of their life. Seven minutes really isn't spending time, nor is it love, because you are not giving anything up at all. You want a sure way to make your child feel forgotten, seven minutes will do the trick. Especially considering that your average male spends up to 50 to 70 hours per week at work. Some will even spend more than that on building a career, which adds up to 10 to 12 hours a day. If you work out those numbers, conservatively speaking, that is a ratio of 1 to 85. For every one minute a father spends with his child, he will spend 85 at work.

Maybe that is why so many kids in our American culture feel forgotten and isolated. Yes, that little blue screen they hold in their hand should incur some of the blame—social media and personal technology do have a mesmerizing quality to them—but you can't fully blame your child's coolness towards you on cell phones and video games alone. I am sure seven minutes also has something to do with it. Sadly, I even know of some dads who spend longer than seven minutes per day on the toilet. Are you not outraged thinking about this number? Seven minutes! May God have mercy on us all.

If you are a dad reading this, before you jump quickly on the defensive, I want you to consider something key in this whole discussion. It is the subject of culpability. Culpability, determining who is most responsible for an action or consequence, always falls on the person who makes the first move. For instance, if a person runs a red light and smashes into another car going through the green light, the person going through the red is always going to be held responsible for the damage. He was the one who made the decision to break the law. He made the first move, or as Rambo with his homespun wisdom puts it, "He drew first blood." Now, with that idea in mind, who is the most culpable for those wild children running around in your house? I know, I know, blame the wife, she is the one who wanted a lot of kids. But my guess is that you, dear sir, are most likely to blame. I am a father of four myself, and being part of the male species, I know that there is an extremely high probability that the physical desire you have for your wife came over you late one night after the lights went out. That means you made the first move.

And since you "drew first blood" you are primarily responsible for those children. You are culpable and you can't get around it! Those wild, crazy-eyed offspring are yours because you started it! And now it is going to take a lifetime for you to finish it. That is why I believe God places a large portion of the responsibility on the father when it comes to raising the children. "Fathers, do not exasperate your children; instead bring them up in the training and instruction of the Lord." (Ephesians 6:4).

So the truth is, you are linked forever with them—they carry your DNA for heaven's sake! The question is, will you be happy about it or play the part of the grumpy, bossy, mean dad? Will you play the poor martyr who is being unfairly saddled with having to care for kids you never wanted? It is your fault! And you better learn to deal with it because it might be the most important part of your life you will have to give account for before Jesus the King. It is sad how many dads treat their children like a bother, as they say, "My kid is a pain in the hind end." With their furrowed brow and grunting disapproval, many men act like it is beneath them to change their son or daughter's diapers. Many manly dads refuse to hold kids when they are fussy, they won't feed them a bottle when they are hungry, and it is too much of a burden to tuck them into bed at night, let alone pray with them. "The game is on," or "I have to watch my news." And God forbid if a father should get up at night to try to calm a screaming baby.

But I was blessed. Not only was my dad happy about having six children to care for and raise, but we were his lifelong hobby.

MORE THAN A HOBBY

What is your hobby? Some men love to fish. They will buy a big boat with all the rigging, fishing poles, lures, high-tech fish finders, a dependable motor, and then pay for the licenses and gas to spend a whole day alone on the lake just to catch a few walleyes or King Salmon. Meanwhile, little Johnny is at home watching television. I know other men who live to work on engines, spending every night and all weekend out in their newly built pole-barn with massive space heaters, just so they can buy a cheap car off of Marketplace, fix it up, and make a few hundred extra dollars reselling it. And baby Sally is shut in the house playing with Ken and Barbie. Other men camp out in the woods for the whole month of November to hunt deer and swill beer with their buddies. And your wife is just trying not to lose her mind picking up dirty underwear and yelling at the boys to get off the video games.

But men work hard all week, don't they have the right to find a little fun for themselves? "All work and no play make Jack a dull boy." You have seen *The Shining*, haven't you? Men need an outlet too, a way to pass leisure time so life is worth living without losing your mind like Jack did. Hobbies are not a bad thing. In fact, God wants us to enjoy living our lives on earth. Though I would say, not all hobbies are profitable. We have been created with purpose after all.

A very curious question we all need to wrestle with is this: Is God going to hold us accountable for how we spend our leisure time or is it simply ours to burn as we see fit? Will the weekend warrior who constantly competes in old-man basketball tournaments all summer long or joins three or four softball leagues be questioned by God how he spent his leisure hours? Is laughing and smiling with our friends at the sand dunes, driving quads and 4-Wheel drive trucks, all God really wants from us? Is spending hours surfing the web or daily binge-watching our favorite television shows how God wants us to spend our lives? Or is there more?

Listen closely to Psalm 127:3-5, "Behold, children are a heritage from the LORD, the fruit of the womb, a reward. Like arrows in the hand of a warrior are the children of one's youth. Blessed is the man who fills his quiver with them! He shall not be put to shame when he speaks with his enemies in the gate."

Somehow, in God's grand design, children are meant to play a big part in a father's life. The word "reward" and "blessed" go hand in hand—children are a gift. And raising them is much more than a hobby, they are strategic tools given to a man to accomplish the will of God on earth. And this is an assignment that requires much more than a mere seven minutes per day.

My dad worked hard at his sales career, extremely hard. But when he was home, he left his work at the office and made it his number one priority to be present for his kids. We were his life, all six of us; four girls and two boys. We meant the world to him. He considered us his pride, joy, and pleasure. Even in the first few months of life, exploring the new world as mumbling, bumbling, drooling, crying babies, he would lay on the living floor and watch us for hours rolling on the carpet or learning how to crawl. He wanted to be there when we took our first steps. It was usually his huge thick hand that held us up as we stood tall, beginning our new life quivering on two legs. It was upon his huge shoulders where we sat as he carried us after we got tired on our long walks in the woods or the local park, or when our tiny legs grew weary in the heat visiting the local zoo.

Some of our fondest memories growing up was when our mom would leave on a women's retreat for a long weekend and our dad would watch us. He would let us do things we normally didn't do during the rest of the week. We would camp out together on a Friday night, sprawled out on the living room floor in our sleeping bags while my dad would make us big paper grocery bags of buttery, homemade popcorn. We also would watch a few movies like *Wizard of Oz* or *Chitty-Chitty, Bang-Bang*, trying to stay up at least until midnight. And then the next day, on Saturday, after a big pancake breakfast, he would have all the neighborhood friends come over for crazy track and field races in our backyard. I will never forget how he would go to the local store and buy a bunch of candy and ice cream sandwiches for "track prizes." So when someone won an event, they got to pick a prize out of the bag. Eventually, he would rig the races so everyone won a prize, even the smallest and skinniest neighbor kid who came to play. It was all about the fun.

DISCIPLINE & DELIGHT

I recently was meeting with a young couple from our church to discuss parenting methods. The mother was extremely distraught as she explained what their home life was like with having two young high-energy kids being cooped up in the house and being married to a husband that was relatively absent when it came to raising them. I asked him why he didn't help out that much and he said, "Because the kids are crazy and they never do what I want them to do!" And then the wife said, wiping tears from her eyes, "How do I get them to behave? At times they don't even want to listen." I looked at them and said, "Is behavior your main goal or is building character? Children are not given to us to perform liked trained seals; they are given to us so we can share our love and delight with them." The young couple looked baffled, "Isn't that our job to get them to obey?" This was the perfect question to explain the importance of delight in the forming of your child's character. So for the next fifteen minutes, I proceeded to explain the fine balance that a parent needs to take when it comes to both discipline and delight.

When it comes to raising children, we all know discipline is a must. You can't have children running the show or believing the sentimental utopian idea that children from birth are pure of heart. Whitney Houston had no idea what she was talking about when she sang the words, "Let the children lead the way." If you believe in the primal perfection of children then you have never seen two small toddlers fight over the same toy, it can quickly turn into World War 3 with straight-up guerilla hand-to-hand combat tactics that include scratching, gouging out eyes, and biting off earlobes. It can get pretty bloody if you are not careful. Civility by force is what a parent is for; to teach, lead, and guide the stubborn heart of the child into the land of mature adulthood.

So of course, we need to teach them discipline. To make it simple, discipline is composed of three qualities: clear communication, a fair punishment that fits the crime, and daily consistency (what is expected of one child must be expected of all). Play no favorites. Proper discipline also includes calmness and steady correction from the parents. Book after parenting book has been written on the necessity of discipline and how to raise an obedient child. Titles such as, *"Have a New Kid by Friday"* or

"Tiger Mom: How you can get your child not only to be successful, but to dominate." It is all about discipline, right?

But there is a path parents can take that is much more important and powerful in the transformation of your child and that is the concept of "delight!" The best way to define delight is treating and communicating to your child, through both words and actions, that you *want* him or her in your life, and that you *like* them. You must communicate that you enjoy his or her person immensely. Look at discipline as the performance of a car, delight is the fuel. You could have the newest model of Ferrari parked in your garage, but if it has no fuel in the tank it goes nowhere. You could also have a fifteen-year-old rusty old beater Chevy Impala in the garage, like I have, and if it has a full tank of gas, we can go places. Delight is high octane, peak performance gasoline for the soul.

Some people will naturally ask the question, "What about showing your child love?" Delight is the visible face of love; it can be seen. It is captured in the smile, the laughter, the hug, the punch in the shoulder, the throwing of the baseball, the taking your daughter to a dance, the sharing of a giant triple-scoop banana split. It says, "You are a wonderful person and I wouldn't want to be with anyone else." When a child believes that they are really wanted by their dad, they find grounding and a lifelong confidence that is rare. David writes about it in Psalm 18:19, "God rescued me because he delighted in me." And when a child is delighted in, they can conquer the world.

SIGNS OF DELIGHT

My dad was a master at delight. If there was one gift he had, it was making my siblings and I know we were liked and wanted. Don't get me wrong, he was still a flawed man who could get angry at the drop of a hat and worked away from home for much of the week, but when he came home, he was with us. He would loosen his tie, take off his shoes, and sit down at the end of the kitchen table. My mom would slide a bowl of salted shelled peanuts in front of him, and we all sat around him cracking peanuts and talked all night long. His questions were usually about us, how we were doing, and what was going on in our life. When you know you are wanted by your father, all the dark shadows of his normal human frailties are quickly burnt away by the bright light of delight.

The delight of a father is best expressed in small ways, not in the big show or over-the-top words that quickly fade away, but in the everyday randomness of life, moment by moment. Small consistent displays of delight help seal up the cracks of doubt that children constantly carry around with them, "I wonder if I am really wanted, and do I bring him pleasure?" So, giving your child a simple nickname like Cramjets or Magic can help them realize they are known in a uniquely special way. Spontaneous trips to the ice cream parlor or a walk in the woods on a sunny Saturday afternoon with our dog were my dad's specialty. Or my favorite part of my friendship with my dad was when he would take me to the newest blockbuster movie so he could blame me for seeing it when he actually wanted to watch it for the second time. "Don," my mom would ask, "why did you take Chris to go see *Close Encounters of the Third Kind*, didn't you already watch it with Gina?"

"Yes," my dad would say, "but he really wanted to see it."

Delight is not that hard, but it has to be genuine. Every son or daughter is equipped with an internal radar system where they can detect real delight from a father that sincerely loves them. Television and talk shows make it seem like dads need to always have deep, emotional conversations if they are going to ever connect with their children, expecting men to be like their wives or a high school counselor who always has some profound insight to share. But God has made the relationship between father and child much more accessible than that because the truth is, all your kids want is your time and attention, laughter and listening, and of course that sideways smile that tells them that they really, really like you.

CONTAGIOUS DELIGHT

One of the results of having a father that delights in his children is that it takes away the tension in the home. You don't need to prove yourself. There are no eggshells that you might unintentionally walk on, and people are allowed to be themselves fully. There is no sarcastic cutting down of each other, and there is no need to compete with who is the best because you know you are already accepted. As a result, not only is your house a refuge from the stress of the world, but people, all kinds of people—strange people, sad people, lonely people—enjoy coming over to see delight firsthand. It is so unusual in most homes. When you are delighted in it, it becomes natural to delight in others.

My friends especially enjoyed coming over to our house. It became the place to be. The moment they would walk through our door my dad would greet them like a long-lost brother, blasting their name in an excited tone, "Lemay! Lemay! So good to see you." Or my friend Bob would hear his favorite nickname, "Skirbs, what's the word?" Instantly a large smile would light across their faces and they would sit down and start talking to my dad because they knew they were welcome. My sister Gina had a meek and mild girlfriend named Sue who was painfully shy, she seemed to be afraid of her own shadow. But after she met my dad and was immediately treated with interest and respect, it only took her a few weeks where she opened right up and completely came out of her shell at our house. My dad liked people, all kinds of people, and they knew it. Even my oldest sister Tammy's hippy-dippy friends with their Cousin It long hair were welcomed! Delight is contagious and my dad was the pied piper of it.

When I finally had some children of my own, they had a visit from my mom and dad for the weekend. We live in Michigan and my parents drove five hours from Cleveland to stay from

Friday through Sunday. It was a warm day in May and when they arrived, I had all the kids come out of the house to welcome them as they pulled up. I gave my mom and dad a hug and then went around to the rear of the car to help grab the luggage and bring it in. It was only a few bags and after I put them in the guest bedroom, I went into the kitchen to join in the conversation that my mom was having with my wife. After a few minutes, I asked mom where dad went. "I don't know," she said, "maybe he's in the bathroom?" But after a few more minutes he still didn't come out.

And then I asked my wife, "Where are all the kids?" She said, "I don't know, they were just here with us." I looked outside and no one was out there, so I headed down into the basement. And there was my dad, sitting on the floor with my three kids, both of the boys were showing him their new video games and my daughter Ginger was hugging him around the neck. Here he was after an exhausting five-hour drive, sitting down in a dark basement playing Nintendo 64 with five and six-year-old boys, while his eight-year-old granddaughter was laughing and talking his ear off. He didn't ignore them or tell them he was too tired to watch a silly video game—he was loving every minute of it. So were they, and that is the point. That is delight in action. It is contagious.

FIVE:
Good Medicine

"They will have no fear of bad news;
their hearts are steadfast, trusting in the Lord."
— *Psalm 112:7*

Life is not easy. Money runs out, bodies wear out, and with some families, as their children get older all they want to do is get out. These thorns and thistles of life can make day-to-day living drudgery if you don't learn how to fight against the fallenness of our human nature. There are too many serious and sad people in the world who go through life like *The Born Loser,* believing that everyone has it out for them. It is just as Titus 3:3 describes, "At one time we too were foolish, disobedient, deceived and enslaved by all kinds of passions and pleasures. We lived in malice and envy, being hated and hating one another." If a person is not careful, and if they don't know how to control their mind or shape their attitude, life can seem like a never-ending journey through a pitch-black labyrinth bordered with prickly bushes of misery while you are daily slogging through knee-deep mud with no hope of daylight.

At least that is how I feel some days, especially when you are writing on a cold dark early February day in Michigan. So, needless to say, I tend to see the glass half-empty. Especially in the morning when I try to pry my heavy body out of bed, I'm often expecting that the nightmares I had the previous night are sure to come true. With my *Chicken Little* mind, it makes it hard for me to want to face another day. I would rather hide under the covers instead of facing the terrible events that are bound to befall me. I have always been that way. Anxiety can be quite crippling.

My dad knew this about me because my dad knew *me*. And because of this, he made it his responsibility to get me out of the dark funk that would often overcome me like a dark shadow. Early in the morning while I was getting ready for work, he would tell me to walk into the bathroom, look in the mirror and say to myself three times loudly, "Boy, am I enthusiastic!" So I would drag my weary bag-o-bones into the bathroom, fighting the whole way, "Dad, I don't want to do that, it makes me feel so stupid."

"Chris," he would say smiling, "it will make you feel like a million bucks. And it is the best way to start the day. Just do it!"

So, with a half-hearted attempt, I would reluctantly say to the grumpy face grimacing back at me in the mirror, "Boy…am I enthusiastic…"

"Louder!" He would say.

I gave a second attempt with a tad more energy, "Boy am I enthusiastic."

"One more time and give it everything you've got!"

"BOY, AM I ENTHUSIASTIC!" I would yell, and without realizing it I began to smile. I didn't want to admit it, but there was something powerful in my Dad's crazy logic. Seeing my smile, he laughed, walked out of the room, and said, "See, you feel a lot better, don't you? Well Chris, have a great day!"

Having a great day is a choice. That is the point he was trying to make. We live in an age where people act as if they have no choice in the outcome of the day, nor in the attitude they want to adopt concerning the events of the day. We have become a nation of victims, always believing we are being taken advantage of. So, if anything bad should happen, things don't go my way, or a person gives me a bad look, we are told it is always someone else's fault. We believe ourselves to be merely passive agents who have no power to fight the dragons of the day. We are led to believe that there is a systemic evil alive and well out there, somewhere, devising nefarious schemes to defeat us. I may not see it, but I know "they" (whoever "they" are), are hidden in the shadows and dark corners of the world trying to ruin my day and make me want to quit like the gate over Hades which reads, "All hope abandon ye who enter here!"

My dad would never allow this attitude to creep too deeply into his kid's heart. He believed we each have been given the ability and power to choose our daily attitude. We can decide either to live in the gutter of misery or exalt in the truth that "This is the day that the Lord has made, let us rejoice and be glad in it."

BEING GLAD

Some may confuse my dad's homespun wisdom with "The Power of Positive Thinking" that was popular in the mid-eighties peddled by Robert Schuler and his ilk. My dad did not believe positivity had any ability in and of itself to change reality—it could not move molecules and make matter bend to a person's desires. Nor did he think if you keep saying something in a positive way that it would come true. But he was a glad person.

Being glad is much different and more effective than positivity, it is how a person courageously reclaims their mind and makes it their own. Gladness believes that God has given me agency to personally decide what thoughts are going to invade the reasoning faculties of my brain, affect my feelings, and hold sway over my decisions. As Proverbs 17:22 says, "A joyful heart is good medicine, but a crushed spirit dries up the bones" A father is primarily responsible for the rejoicing that will totally transform the atmosphere of the home. Even when all seems bleak and lost, good dads must still remind their wives and children that God has not abandoned us. Grace is always available.

Being glad is a precarious task, it is not for the faint of heart. There are two dangerous cliffs of emotional extremes that we can easily fall from if a person is not careful. On one cliff is forced positivity. That is when all of life becomes a fake, happy charade. If not careful, forced positivity can turn into a sugary sweet poison that is of no use to anyone when navigating through the real, painful difficulties of everyday life. Ignoring actual pain while wearing a plastered-on smile is not genuine gladness, it is actually cruel indifference. On the other cliff is bitter cynicism. If you don't work hard to enjoy the day that the Lord has made, the deceitfulness of the human heart easily slides to negativity and doubt. Bitter cynicism betrays a lack of trust in the goodness of God. It takes real talent to bring joy into your world that is real. Jesus had it. Hebrews 1:9 talks about Jesus by saying,

"God, your God, has anointed you
with the oil of gladness beyond
your companions."

Jesus excelled above every man in joy. I know he is known as the "suffering servant", "a man of sorrows", and the "slain lamb", but it was all for joy. Listen to Hebrews 12:2, "Looking to Jesus, the founder and perfecter of our faith, who for the joy that was set before him endured the cross, despising its shame." Jesus did all things for the joy, maintaining a hidden wonder and expecting the hand of God to direct and provide for you. It is this kind of attitude in life that undergirds how we embrace the day today and look forward to a future joy that is waiting for us—a real heaven with a happy God for our Father. Jesus didn't suffer just to suffer; his suffering was laced with hope. His news is good news, his weapon is agape love.

Never did Jesus allow bitterness, anger, despondency, and cynicism to define him. He wasn't like your average American male who thinks masculinity is living as a stoic "Desperado." As

Don Henley describes it in the song by the same name, "O you're a hard one, but I know you have your reasons." I think society's obsession and pushback against toxic masculinity is nothing more than the obvious recognition that the macho man who has no joy is really not much of a man after all.

Jesus was never known for being stern or acting like he was distracted by more important things in life that only a man can understand. He was kind, sensitive, had time for small people, and lived in constant joy. He could rejoice in the moment because he knew God His Father was always in control. And even during his seasons of pain—and he faced real, severe, pain—there always was a contagious joy that was bubbling just beneath the surface.

Fathers need to acquire and then communicate this to those they love. If they don't, who will? You aren't a man because you have important business to take care of. Your stern seriousness when building an addition on your house, or acting like you can't be disturbed while cutting the grass with your new zero-turn John Deere mower, is not that impressive. Anybody can be a cold-hearted loner, there is nothing to be proud of in that. Calloused indifference does not define a real man—gladness and joy does. And laughter will be abundant. It will flow from you, for it is the language of hope. A dad that can offer these things to his family will always have on hand sweet medicine that he can freely administer into the bloodstream of your needy children's souls. My dad understood this.

STORIES OF LAUGHTER

I once heard that the stories you tell that cause your children to laugh at the dinner table teach them more about life and lasts longer than any of the lessons they learn at church or school. Our family spent a lot of time laughing around our table and I can remember endless stories that caused us to have a good belly-busting laugh. Let me mention just three priceless stories that will never leave me:

Our family lived in a large three-story English Tudor house that had an old furnace system with steel radiators placed in every room to heat them up. To fully heat such a large house and reach every room cost a lot of money. And to make matters worse, we lived directly across the street from Lake Erie, the shallowest of the Great Lakes which froze over with thick ice almost every winter. So where we lived got cold—frigid cold—and to supplement the cost of running the furnace, my dad decided to buy bags of coal to burn in the fireplace. He would often purchase bags of coal to have on hand before we lost power or it was an extremely cold night, so he would have a number of bags stored in the garage.

I remember one particular time when he was excited because he found a good deal on bags of coal that were half off, so he splurged and bought about ten of the bags. A few weeks later, a winter storm hit and the power in our house went out. My dad was excited as this was the perfect time for him to burn some of the coal he bought. So, our family all gathered around the fireplace and sat on our matching green velvet couches underneath thick blankets, getting ready to warm up with this new cost-efficient coal my dad bought. He put two bags in, lit them, and we all watched the fire burn hot!

There we were, my four sisters, my brother and I, and my mom and dad snuggling together under blankets in the pitch dark watching the coal in the fireplace burn. It was fun staying warm while we listened to my dad tell stories of long ago and hearing my sisters laughing at each tall tale. The warm glow of the flickering flames reflected off of our smiling faces and twinkling lively eyes. After a couple of hours, my mom wondered if the power turned on because she heard beeping in the kitchen, so she went in and checked the lights. When she switched the overhead light on it immediately flashed on and my mom gasped in horror. The whole house was covered in an inch of black coal dust!

My mom looked at her sleeves and hands and they also had a layer of oily soot. She went into the bathroom to look at her face and said she looked like Bert; the chimney sweep played by Dick Van Dyke in Mary Poppins. "Don!" She yelled, "Turn on the lights, you won't believe it!"

My dad stood up and ran over to the living room light switch and flashed on all the lights. He gasped and a mischievous grimace was displayed across his face. There sat our whole family, blanketed in a swirling cloud of thick black dust. Our shag carpet was black, our blankets were black, our couches were black, our hair was black, our dog was black, and everything was dusted black like ink because the coal my dad bought was not meant for indoors. My dad then smiled at all of us looking like we were dipped in tar and said, "No wonder that darn coal was so cheap!" He then he started laughing. Uproarious laughter that he couldn't contain. My sister's shock at what they saw quickly turned to laugher, my brother and I laughed. I loved it when my brother laughed. Even though we knew we had some major clean-up to do, that cold winter day is a day that I will never forget.

Another time of gladness was during a hot summer Saturday. My mom called all of us kids in for a quick lunch of hotdogs, potato chips, and large triangle-cut slices of watermelon. My dad was trimming the hedges and said he was almost finished and would be in shortly, so we all gathered around the kitchen table, silently chowing down. It was a lazy uneventful day. Ten minutes later, my dad came in and the first thing he did is grab a piece of watermelon. This was in the seventies so local grocery stores didn't sell seedless watermelons, which means every watermelon sold still had large black seeds in them. After taking a big bite out of the juicy fruit, my dad began spitting the black seeds at my siblings and me.

"Don, what are you doing?" My mom yelled. My dad said nothing but continued spitting watermelon seeds and soon a large black seed landed directly on the middle of my astonished mother's forehead. We knew he was in trouble so we tried not to laugh, but we couldn't help it. Soon seeds were flying from everywhere. My sisters spit them at my dad, my brother spit them at my sisters, and I shot a few at my dog, Ellie Poo.

My mom knew this was a helpless situation, so she too grabbed a piece and started spitting them at my dad. After a good ten minutes, black seeds were everywhere, the white patterned wallpaper now had a polka-dotted pattern of black seeds. My dad did it again—he turned an average quiet summer Saturday was into a seed-fest of hilarity we would never forget.

The final episode of laughter that I am going to share was carried out completely at my expense. At the time, I was not happy, but looking back I can say confidently that it was exactly what a chronic mopey boy like me needed.

I was heading home after a long baseball practice which was located kitty-corner across the street from our house. My family knew that my normal routine was to jump my neighbor's backyard fence to get to my yard, which then led into our house through the back door to our laundry room, where I would take off my dirty uniform. So, without my knowledge, my dad and sisters were hiding above the backdoor of our house equipped with two large buckets full of cold tap water that they were getting ready to drop on my head. My dad planned this dark deed with full cooperation from my devious sisters, Steph and Gina, who loved to pull practical jokes on their unsuspecting little brother.

The ledge they were hiding behind was on a flat patio that was perfectly situated for a backdoor ambush. As I was getting close to the door, I put my dusty baseball glove and aluminum bat in my left hand so I could use my right to grab the handle of the back door. The moment my hand touched the metal bar of the door handle, an ice-cold stream of water accosted me from above. I looked up and saw three sinister faces laughing at my soggy predicament.

After catching her breath from heavy laughter, my sister Steph cried out loud, "Dad, we got him, perfect hit!" I was furious. And I was not in a mood to talk to anyone. I was tired, hungry, and soaking wet! So I did what every pouting little brother would do—I threw down my bat and glove, and said, "I am running away from home!" Then I sprinted back to the fence I just jumped over, leapt over it again, and headed to the baseball field I just left. When I got there, I climbed all the way up the large backstop and laid on top of the over-arching part of the aluminum fencing and told myself then and there I was never going back home.

So there I stayed, arms folded tight across my chest while I stared up into the blue sky, lying on my back on the backstop fence. "I'll show them!" I muttered to myself. Five minutes passed and there I was, all by my angry self. The metal bands of the fence were starting to dig into my back, but I was not budging. Ten minutes went by and I was convinced that my refusal to come home was the harshest punishment I could mete out on my dad and sisters. They were probably repenting of how they cruelly ambushed me, and I was sure they were overwhelmed with guilt and shame about the way they always treated me.

A half-an-hour went by and I sat up looking for any sign of remorse and repentance from my family, but nothing. And man was my butt getting sore from that stupid fence. This running away business is not what I thought it was cracked up to be. And why isn't my family coming to apologize and beg for forgiveness? No longer angry as I originally was, I grew increasingly tired of my ill-conceived plan, but I had to save face and keep up the fight. "Chris," I told myself, "Don't quit. They will eventually give in."

I then saw my sister Steph crossing the street heading my way. *Aha, here she comes, I knew it!* My stubborn courage kicked back into high gear and I was not going to be moved. *I am going to make sure she knows just how mad I am.*

"Hey Chris, come on down, it is time for dinner!" Steph yelled up.

"I'm not coming down." I grumped back at her. "I told you, I am running away from home."

"Suit yourself, it's Chef Boyardee Pizza Night. If you don't come home now, I'm sure Donny is going to eat your slices!" Oh yeah, it was pizza night, I forgot! That was one of my favorite meals, especially the way my mom made it. Melted cheese and pepperoni with crunchy Lay's potato chips on the side and sweet Lipton's iced tea to wash it all down. My mouth was watering and my fury subsided. "Steph, wait up! I'm coming!"

Coming into the kitchen my mom told me to wash my hands before I sat down. After all my siblings and I were sitting, my dad prayed, and we said, "Amen." Then we each grabbed two pieces of pizza and began to eat. Boy was it good. "Hey Chris, how did that running away from home thing go?" My dad asked with a small grin.

"I decided it was a bad idea," I said.

"Well, you sure got mad," Gina said, "and boy was your face red." She laughed, Steph laughed, Tammy laughed, my dad and brother laughed, my mom laughed, and after taking another bite of pizza, so did I. Being home was so much better than running away, even if I had some water poured on my head. I eventually dried out, my belly was full, and I thought to myself, "Maybe it was all in good fun." Toward the end of the meal, my dad said, "Hey Chris, the Indians are on tonight, you want to watch it with me?" I looked at him and said, "I would love to. Can I have that last piece of pizza mom?" "Sure, my dear." She replied, as she handed me the final piece.

GETTING OVER YOURSELF

What my dad helped all of us to do was to not take everything so personally. He wanted us to learn to laugh at ourselves, even a good-natured prank needed to be enjoyed and not turned into a sign that you have been victimized. I began to learn that family pranks and kind-hearted kidding around were a way to show that you were part of the family—that you were noticed and enjoyed. And in another sense, it also showed me that I wasn't all that important. The world didn't revolve around me. If a person couldn't learn to look past insults, it was a sure sign they were too proud to laugh.

People are far too serious these days precisely because they take themselves and their importance so seriously. In an eggshell world nothing is funny anymore. But true gladness looks past hurts and gives people the benefit of the doubt. The mature person has the grace to forgive other's failures and even faults. And because of that, life is not so heavy, it is light. If hope floats, gladness sails by.

I have found that only those who can forgive can actually laugh. Those who can't are keeping records of wrongs and looking to be offended. A cheerful heart is more than good medicine, it makes life easy. My dad taught me that.

SIX:
Finding God

Suppose I go to the Israelites and say to them,
'The God of your fathers has sent me to you,' and they ask me,
'What is his name?' Then what shall I tell them?"
God said to Moses, "I am who I am."
— *Exodus 3:13-14*

No one really knows a person's relationship with another. And this is especially true with the infinite Almighty God because his ways are beyond us. The Scriptures are crystal clear about Jehovah's mysterious will and the covert operations that he is intimately involved in from day to day.

Paul says, "Oh, the depth of the riches and wisdom and knowledge of God! How unsearchable are his judgments and how inscrutable his ways! For who has known the mind of the Lord, or who has been his counselor?" And consider the words of Isaiah, "For my thoughts are not your thoughts, neither are your ways my ways." And even Jesus makes this profoundly stealthy comment, "You must be born again. The wind blows where it wishes, and you hear its sound, but you do not know where it comes from or where it goes. So it is with everyone who is born of the Spirit." God does what he is going to do, and he never needs anyone's permission to do it.

And yet, in our blind pride and incorrigible arrogance, human beings believe that they can correctly detail God's precise movements. We actually think we can predict what he is up to and that we have the capability to decode the mind of God. So, while seeing through a glass darkly, we devise elaborate theological charts, graphs, and theories all in the effort of pinpointing how the infinite invisible transcendent God chooses where, how, and why he does the things he does. And then after all of our calculating and blustering sophistry, we give out silly cookie-cutter advice on how to unlock eternity and procure eternal blessings for ourselves as if it were all a matter of mathematics. And yet most of us tend to forget that when you try to pour the untamable living God into a human-sized bottle you will always fall profoundly short. We are far too easily impressed with our own reasoning.

But there is one thing we do know; God is about the business of seeking and finding the lost. He wants people to want him, he is on the hunt for humans. And if you were to open your spiritual eyes and look closely at the small events taking place every single day, he leaves an abundance of clues and breadcrumbs that show us he has been hunting for each of us. But how he captures an individual human heart is the grandest mystery of them all, precisely because his strategy seems to change depending on the person he is trying to catch.

Take my dad for instance. His relationship with the Creator of the Universe had some of the strangest twists and turns I have ever seen, but in the end, God got him. God always gets his man. God knew my dad is naturally stubborn, so it takes some real doing to get my dad to give up and admit defeat. God had to work hard to pin my dad on the spiritual wrestling mat, and like Jacob, once my dad was engaged, he wouldn't let go until he was blessed. As his son, I had a front row seat to watch this intense grappling match. I saw the pain that is required for God to humble a man, and I also witnessed the highs a person experiences when they finally possess genuine faith. A true relationship with God includes pain, joy, confusion, heartache, and ecstasy; when God is chasing you down and buying back your lost soul, he will use any means necessary to obtain it. Through my dad, I got to see all of this, and it is always amazing how the perfect God will condescend in grace and mercy to love us flawed human beings.

RELIGION AIN'T SO BAD

Tradition these days has been given a bad rap. The popular thing to do in our cynical postmodern age is to share sordid stories about how the old and outdated patriarchal systems of hierarchy and large institutions of religion have done nothing but harm the poor and innocent. We are masters at historical deconstruction. People are now using religion as a whipping post for their own spiritual failures and faults. It is second nature for us to blame the old, white-bearded men in robes and claim they are the ones who have caused people not to believe in God. There is this false belief that the gatekeepers for God are composed of the good old boy clubs of leadership, so let's put the blame on them for why faith has failed for most. That is the easy way out.

But this was not true for my dad, he loved growing up in the structure, the beauty, and the sights and sounds that the traditional church offered. He would say that the consistency of the liturgy and solemnity of the mass was a needed antidote to our wishy-washy world of relativity that has no stable foundation or conviction to build a moral life. He cherished the memories that were made amongst the community of saints and felt serving God in the church was a delightful duty.

So, as he raised his large young family, he knew that it was his job to bring us to church. We learned to sing songs to a majestic Father, and we were taught that Jesus was indeed the Savior of the World. Easter, Christmas, First Communion, Ash Wednesday, Palm Sunday, and other important days on the church calendar were times for the whole family to dress up and make God important. He encouraged his boys to wear itchy sweaters and sports coats out of respect, and my sisters wore dresses because church was to be a grand event—a time to celebrate and worship in our best attire.

After mass, he would invite his mom and dad, nearby cousins, and even friends and neighbors from the church to come over and enjoy the day by celebrating Christ as a family. It was important to him to plan the calendar of events around God.

He wanted to be a part of God's witness on earth. It was strongly imprinted in him, much more so than most men in the community. I don't know how to explain it, but for my dad, God was really real and he wanted us to have him in our life as well. He made Sundays a priority so God would be real to us too; we had to go to mass even when we didn't want to go.

There was a time when my brother Don, a budding philosopher and young contrarian by nature, refused to go to mass because on that particular Sunday he wasn't sure he believed and he wanted to stay true to his convictions. My dad said to him, "Don, if you are going to live in this house you are going to go with the family to church, even if you sit in the car in the parking lot, you are still going." And so he did. I can still see my brother with an angry countenance and arms crossed, sitting in the back seat of our paneled station wagon, while the rest of us attended mass. When the church was open, my dad wanted to be there.

There was another occasion when I had to stay home from church because I had a seriously high fever. My dad took the rest of the family to church while my mom stayed home with me. When they got back my dad came into the living room where I was resting on the couch to see how I was doing. He propped my hot head up on a few pillows and said, "Chris, I know I am not supposed to do this, but I went up to communion twice so I could get you a communion wafer." He pulled out his white handkerchief and wrapped inside was a small circular communion wafer that my dad snuck out of the church for me. He grabbed a small cup of wine from the kitchen, then kneeling next to me, he administered communion. "Chris, this is the body of Christ." I said, "Amen" and then took the wafer and ate it. "Chris, this is the blood of Christ." I said, "Amen" and then took the cup and drank. I know that the church would frown on what my dad did, but he didn't want me to miss a chance at participating in worship.

I learned later that my dad even felt compelled to dig deeper into the mystery of knowing God, so he attended all the new movements that the church had to offer. He went to a weekend retreat with other men and learned for the first time that according to the Bible, God wanted us to live by faith and not just duty and sacrament. He told me later that in 1968 he prayed to God and asked to be made "born again." This was a phrase that was not often used in the traditional church circles we attended. He said he knew that the Spirit of God took residence in his heart that day and he was forever compelled by his new love for Jesus.

I will never forget one Easter brunch around the dinner table when my dad got into a heated discussion with his mom, who was also very religious. I was sitting at the kid's table with my sisters, and my grandma who was at the adult table said, "Don, why don't you pray to the saints and Mary like you used to?" His response was, "Why pray to the saints and Mary when you have Jesus in your life? Isn't he enough?" My Grandma, who was feisty and a steadfast defender of tradition, slammed down her fork on the table and vehemently replied, "Don, Mary is Jesus' mother, don't disrespect her." My dad was determined, "But Ma, Jesus alone is God. Mary was still a human. She can't do anything for me."

Wow! Was my grandma mad. But that was a pivotal moment for me because I saw in my dad's faith a sure conviction founded in Jesus alone. He was God and that was enough. End of discussion. I learned then and there that my dad wasn't into religion, he was into truth. He wanted to know what was really real. Sure, the pomp and circumstance that surrounded the mass and the tradition was beautiful, even helpful, but it was the person behind it that mattered most.

CRISIS OF FAITH

My dad always claimed to be a simple man. He was moved more by passion and love for Jesus than getting caught up in doctrinal word splitting and theological debates. He knew God was alive, his Son was Jesus Christ, and the Holy Spirit lived in him and that was enough. He rarely questioned the church he went to because he knew he still could find God there. He would often say it was your own fault if you didn't get anything out of the mass. But God had other plans for my dad than religious contentment, he wanted more of him. And when God wants more of a person, he uses a season of difficult testing so that the person being tested will reach out and find him. My dad was that man.

The night of God's new movement toward my dad and his family will be forever etched in my memory. I was sitting at the kitchen table with my mom reading a book while my mom was feeding my sister Laura a small dinner before she got her ready for bed, a normal uneventful evening was already underway. It was dark outside and we were simply doing what we normally would do waiting for my dad to get home so we could eat dinner together.

After I read a few chapters from my book and sipped down a few splashes from a can of Diet Coke, I noticed a large, silhouetted outline of my dad approaching the sliding doors that led into the kitchen. Before he came into the house, he stood in the darkness for about a minute wiping his eyes, and when he opened the slider and finally came into the light of the kitchen you could instantly see from the look on his face that something was wrong, terribly wrong. His posture was heavy and hunched and his eyes had a faraway look, there was also a hint of shock and total defeat. The pain I could see in his eyes caught my attention most. They were bloodshot and swollen, still filled with moisture, and I knew he was crying for quite a while before coming to the door.

My mom saw it too, "Don, what is the matter?" She dropped the spoon she was using to feed Laura, stood up and grabbed my dad's briefcase, then told him to sit down.

My dad slowly slumped onto one of the kitchen chairs, not bothering to take off his dark blue overcoat, and announced, "I have been fired." With a look of bewilderment, he continued, "Out of the clear blue they fired me. They told me to grab all my things because they hired someone else for my position. It's over, I was a National Sales Manager for only three lousy months, and now it is done."

We were all in shock. There we sat, no one said a word for the next five minutes while my dad dropped his head into his hands. My mom couldn't hold in her outrage, "Don, how could they do this to you? You worked your butt off for that company. I don't understand!" And then she made a quick comment born from the frustration exploding from her heart, "And how could God allow this to happen? You have been faithful to him all your life? Why, Don, why?"

My dad looked up, but instead of holding onto the despair he came in with, a fierce resolve came over his face, "Rita, this is not God's fault. We can't praise God when things go well and then blame him when they go bad, we need to understand what he is doing. Because he is always up to something." He then turned to me, "Chris, go get a bible, we are going to figure this out together as a family."

Something forever changed that day in my dad's heart. The loss of his job was the new spark that God used to rejuvenate his faith. He was now in hot pursuit of the Living God. Being fired at the age of 55 completely obliterated his pride. But it also forced his hand to find God afresh. For most of his life religion was a wonderful way to live, it was the right thing to do, it gave a great foundation for his family to build their lives up, but it wasn't enough. God wanted my dad, and for the first time, my dad only wanted to know God and his unvarnished truth. In order to build my dad's faith, God had to wreck the years my dad spent building his beautiful framework of religion and tradition. It was hard to watch, gut-wrenching at times, but God knew it was what my dad needed. Jesus was on the hunt for Don Weeks, and he caught him.

GOLD MINING

I have learned that when miners go searching for gold, they look for large "veins of gold" that are trapped in quartz and granite formed from cataclysmic events like earthquakes or underground fault lines when high-pressure water pushes up reserves of gold that were hiding deep in the earth. And once a vein is found in the rock, you have struck it rich. A giant vein of gold, known as the "Mother Lode", can lead to untold quantities of gold. I think when God goes searching for people, he looks for that "vein of gold"—the believer who will lead to many more.

In the book of Acts there is a fascinating story that is found in chapter 16 where Paul and Silas are locked in a jail and an earthquake happens. It says that the jail warden who was responsible for keeping the prisoners locked up was sleeping and awoke after the earthquake and saw that the prison doors were left wide open. He assumed that all the prisoners escaped. Right when he was about to kill himself for failing in his responsibility—he must have been under some incredible personal pressure and anxiety to be willing to take his own life—Paul shouted to him, "Stop! Don't kill yourself! We are all here!"

The jailer was stunned. He couldn't believe that the men wouldn't bolt and so he turned to Paul and said, "What must I do to be saved?" He must have heard the gospel from Paul earlier and he wanted answers concerning his soul. He was hungry for God. The next part in Acts 16:31 is fascinating. Paul replied, "Believe in the Lord Jesus Christ and you will be saved, along with everyone in your household." In other words, this jail warden was a "vein of gold." Through his miraculous conversion after the earthquake, he believed, and so did his family. This is exactly how God worked in our family.

For my dad, losing his job was the earthquake that changed his life. And he became the "vein of gold" that led to a mother lode of faith for our family.

A few weeks after the incident in the kitchen my dad turned to me and said, "Your mom and I have decided to switch churches. We realized that we were not properly taught the Bible at our old church, and that just doesn't cut it anymore. We found a place where the pastor preaches straight truth, the Bible is actually studied over the old traditions and silly superstitions that are invented by men. Would you like to join us?" I was hesitant at first, but soon I followed my dad's lead and started falling in love with the scriptures as well.

All three of us, my mom, my dad, and I, began making up for years of lost time. We couldn't get enough of God's word. My mom ordered tapes on the radio from every Bible teacher she could get her hands on; Dr. J. Vernon McGee, Charles Swindol, David Jeremiah, and Chuck Smith from Calvary Chapel, and the list goes on. My parents joined small group Bible studies which lead to more bible studies, and they even became Bible study leaders for the next 10 years.

I became obsessed with knowing scripture and theology. I was blown away by the doctrine of "Justification by faith alone." I can remember reading a book in my bedroom that talked about how faith in Christ was the only way to have peace with God. And once I believed, all my sins, past, present, and especially future sins, were covered by the blood of Christ. I was overwhelmed. I ran downstairs and said, "Dad! Dad! Did you know that if you believe in Jesus all your sins are completely paid for? Even the ones you are going to commit tomorrow!" My dad smiled and said, "Chris, I have been trying to tell you that for years now. But God needed to show you his grace because the Holy Spirit has to be the one to open your eyes to the truth."

My dad was never financially restored to where he was before he lost his job. For the next fifteen years, he struggled to even find a job that was close to comparable compensation to what he made in sales. In fact, he and my mom eventually had to sell their large house that he bought when he moved to the east side of Cleveland to take the National Sales Manager job and they were forced to buy a much smaller ranch house they could afford. But the newfound joy he and my mom had in Christ was more than they could ever ask for or imagine. Through the crushing of my dad, God found his "vein of gold."

In the immediate years after the loss of his job, all my dad's children made a profound profession of faith in Christ. My oldest sister Tammy started bringing her family to a large church to be raised under clear Bible teaching. My brother Don was called to be a missionary to Bolivia and he eventually became a pastor in West Virginia. My sister Regina took the gospel into the jails of Southern California where she uses her gifts to disciple broken women and lead them to Jesus. My sister Steph joined a new church plant on the West Side of Cleveland where she and her husband are consistently asked to take on important leadership roles. And the youngest of the brood, me, went to Russia to teach the Bible in public schools and I have been pastoring in the apple country of Michigan for the last 25 years.

You could say when my dad lost his job he found God, but the truth is, God found him.

SEVEN:
The Unanswered Prayer

"All these people were still living by faith when they died.
They did not receive the things promised; they only saw them and
welcomed them from a distance, admitting that they were
foreigners and strangers on earth."
— *Hebrews 11:13*

"Don't Tread on Me" has been seared into freedom-loving Americans from birth. One of the hardest lessons for a person growing up in this country is to learn that you are not in charge. For the last 250 years, Americans have been swimming in the democratic waters of independence and liberty. We don't like to be told what to do and we carry a natural distrust for any kind of authority. We take great national pride in saying that our forefathers would not bow to the English king. We are not accustomed to singing "God Save the Queen", and even our boss' in the workplace have to give us good reason for us to do their bidding. Leave us alone so we can go it on our own, and with just a little bit of grit, sweat, and ingenuity, the American dream of success and prosperity is right at your fingertips.

My father was the embodiment of the all-American self-made man. Through hard work, charm, and an incredible ability to connect with people, he grew to be a highly successful businessman. When it came to sales, he always exceeded his monthly quotas, winning award after award. He would take great pride in his ability to close the deal. "Chris," he would say, "true salespeople are more than order takers, they are persuaders and influencers." And there was a great thrill when he could get the toughest customer to sign on the dotted line. My mom lost count on how many trips he won through his company where he was able to take her to places like Hawaii, Charleston, South Carolina, a few cruises on the Caribbean, Hong Kong, China, and they even took a trip to England and Ireland where she got to sip a cool beer at a local pub.

One of our favorite perks of his job was when he brought home all the new appliances that came out on the market. We were the first family to have a microwave oven on the street. We would invite the neighborhood kids over to watch us blow up hotdogs and melt plastic forks in the new-fangled magical appliance. He even brought home a refrigerator with an ice cream maker. It made the best natural strawberry and vanilla flavors you have ever tasted. I can still remember the sweetness of the strawberry thirty years later.

He was always amazing us. I can remember when he came home a bit early from a trip out of town and he drove up to our driveway with the newest and fastest rental car that was available in the Hertz lot. "I won a few days of free car rentals and I could bring home whichever one I wanted, so I thought you guys would like to drive the newest Pontiac Firebird." He would then toss me the keys to drive around the neighborhood to show off. "Chris, give it a little gas!" He would say, and I would press down on the gas pedal while the car would roar down our nice, respectable suburban neighborhood, impressing all the dads who were outside cutting their lawns. As we drove by, he would lean the passenger car seat back and suck in his cheeks like James Dean from Rebel Without a Cause.

Even when it came to working around the house, he had a strange knack for keeping things humming right along. He could build small additions to the house, Bondo a rusted-out car door, and of course, he could repair almost anything with a roll of good duct tape. He was no master craftsman, but he somehow could find a way around any problem. My mom wanted some bookshelves for all of her Harlequin novels, so he made a four-tiered, wall-to-wall shelving unit that was very impressive. He even had an art easel in the basement where he would quickly paint an outdoor nature scene out of oils and acrylics to match the new color decor that my mom wanted for the living room. And to top it all off, he could sing like Frank Sinatra and had striking dark features that reminded many of my friends of Elvis.

He was truly a talented man, and as his son, I thought he could do no wrong. I even remember playing H.O.R.S.E. with him on our basketball court and I couldn't seem to beat him. After he thrashed my brother and I in a game of cut-throat pool down in our basement, my brother told me he always would win because he knew how to play his "old man mind tricks" against us. He seemed to delight in trying to psych us out. I would often ask him, "Dad, how come you always beat me in basketball, ping-pong, and pool?" and he said, "Chris, it is all mind over matter." Then with a smile and a wink he would joke, "I don't mind, and you don't matter."

If there ever was an award for "The Most Interesting Man in the World" I am convinced he would be the perfect candidate. He was a very independent and confident man. However, there is one thing that he never could fix, my sister Laura.

LITTLE LAURA LEE *

Somewhere around the age of 16 months, my sister Laura Lee, his second child, had a brain that started to malfunction. For her whole first year of life, she was like any other baby; she would smile at my mom's face, laugh at my dad's tickling, and grab for the same toys her baby brother Donny wanted. And boy did she love Mary Poppins! My dad would often play a 33 RPM vinyl record which contained all the musical numbers from the film. And when he played "I Love to Laugh" Laura would stop everything she was doing and smile, holding up her chubby little fist in glee.

And then, without warning, without reason, some of the wiring in her body started shorting out. This lovely child who was born in New Orleans—we pronounced her name as Lara because my mom said she was the only southern bell in the family— stopped responding to the world around her. Her mind went blank and her body started revolting against nature with terrifying violence. Her tender little frame was rendered helpless to oncoming bouts of random seizures, violent rocking, and a continual wringing of her hands.

As the symptoms increased, my mom and dad desperately looked for help. Taking her to numerous doctors and neurologists, they searched for answers. Any answers. But none could be given. For two grueling years, my parents made hundreds of calls, drove to various hospitals, and looked for any solution to help find a cure for their small fragile daughter.

But none could be found.

Day after day my sweet sister slipped deeper and deeper into her rusty cage. A prisoner to a body that no longer worked.

Her condition is known as Rett syndrome. From the official correspondence of the Rett organization, it is found to be a "rare genetic neurological disorder that occurs almost exclusively in girls and leads to severe impairments, affecting nearly every aspect of the child's life: their ability to speak, walk, eat, and even breathe easily. The hallmark of Rett syndrome is near constant repetitive hand movements."

Laura was a daddy's girl; my father considered her well-being his responsibility. Not only would he keep feeding her at the dinner table long after the rest of us kids were done eating, small bite after small bite, but he never gave up hope for a cure. It was his voice she responded to. He would come into the room and say, "Hey Laura, how are you girl?" She would crinkle her eyes and blow out a small amount of pent-up air from her lungs as her rock got faster.

She knew her dad.

Sometimes he would have all of us sing to her some of her favorite songs, "Little Laura Lee", and "Tiny Bubbles" by Don Ho. But when we all sang "I Love to Laugh" something inside her brain fired. Like an old Chevy truck trying to crank over and come alive, Laura's eyes sparked. For a short few seconds you could catch a smile—Laura actually smiled! It wasn't a full wide-awake smile, but it was a faint far-away smile like she was holding a secret only she knew. As if she was trying to tell us all that a better day was coming.

Laura was also my father's partner in crime. When he wanted to get a reaction from my friends at the dinner table he would feed Laura some of the messiest food he could find. The worst of all was watermelon. After each bite of the pink fruit, my sister would drool juice like a waterfall. You couldn't help but look at the chunky liquid that oozed out from her mouth, and as Laura chewed my dad acted like he didn't notice the large, goopy mess she made. He would tie a big towel around her neck, and to the surprise of my friends, they would gawk as she would slobber and spit. They didn't want to be rude so they didn't say a thing, but my sisters and I couldn't hold in the hilarity.

My dad's bible was filled with constant prayers for Laura. His favorite verses were dated alongside prayers of petition concerning her, "Lord please heal Laura." Again and again, a father's longing for the health of his girl was recorded. Days, months, and years he wrote his requests for his dear girl to have a normal life. But alas, there was no answer in sight.

The self-made, successful, charming, talented man was rendered helpless. He couldn't fix the daughter that he loved. God used a sweet harmless soul to break the pride of my dad. "Why wasn't God healing her?" He would ask. "Do we not have enough faith?" Questions about my sister's condition haunted him most of his life.

A BLESSING IN DISGUISE

The toughest question for people who love God usually revolves around unanswered prayer. The logic usually goes like this; If God is good, why does he allow so much suffering and pain? Or, He tells us to pray and if you pray in his name you will receive, but since I am not getting the answer, I want I must not be praying right. Through my sister's condition, and my dad's years and years of spiritual struggle, I have realized that God teaches us things through unanswered prayer that we would learn no other way:

- How to Love Unconditionally
- Cherishing the Sanctity of Human Life
- Perseverance through Trials

- Seeing the Difference in Suffering as Compared to Inconvenience

Though all these lessons are important to consider, the one thing I think my dad taught me about watching your daughter crushed by a cruel disease, is that none of us are in control. As much as we want to be, we are not in charge, we don't call the shots—God does. Even with my dad's determination and talent he still couldn't do a thing. The condition of my sister Laura was way beyond him and he had to trust in someone higher and mightier than himself.

Redemption and resurrection of the body is the true miracle, not finding health and prosperity here on earth. Yes, those things are gifts and wonderful blessings from God, but someday it will all be taken away. And if all your hope is resting on the here and now, it will never be secure. We know it won't last. Rust and moth rule, health breaks down, teeth fall out, and for my sister, she lost everything at the tender age of two. From a human perspective, she was robbed. She never got to experience the things the rest of her siblings enjoyed. She never had her first kiss, won a race, or enjoyed making strawberry ice cream in the new ice cream maker dad brought home.

Heaven was more real to my dad because of my sister though. He acquired a genuine hunger for eternity the more the years rolled by with no healing for Laura. He also knew that waiting up in the new Eden were the answers to all his prayers concerning Laura. Having a broken daughter was not a permanent state; her disease kept him tethered to the eternal things, the real things. Even the taste for accumulating possessions and making a name for yourself, which is a snare for most people, held no pull or promise for him. Like the cheap trinkets you can win at a local carnival, my dad saw new cars, nice clothes, and fancy houses in the same way. All sparkle and glitter that lasts for a few short moments are nothing compared to the unshakable kingdom God offers us in eternity.

Who could ever imagine such a wretched disease could end up being such a powerful blessing? Psalms 16:9-11 captures the true believer's heavenly anticipation:

> *"Therefore, my heart is glad and my tongue rejoices;*
> *my body also will rest secure,*
> *because you will not abandon me to the realm of the dead,*
> *nor will you let your faithful one see decay.*
> *You make known to me the path of life;*
> *you will fill me with joy in your presence,*
> *with eternal pleasures at your right hand."*

A WORLD WITHOUT BLAME

One Sunday, a very pious couple came up to my dad after church because they wanted to talk to him about my sister Laura. They had very serious faces and very earnest hearts, "We have heard about the condition of your daughter and we want to pray for healing for her. We believe that God wants to do an amazing miraculous work in her life. Can we come over and share what God has laid on our hearts?" My dad said, "Sure, I will never turn down prayers."

The next Saturday, the husband and wife came into our house and asked to see Laura with the rest of our family gathered around. They were wearing very plain clothes, like Mennonites, both had well-worn bibles in their hands, and they were also holding a plastic bag full of audiotapes. Once we were all in the living room, Laura was wheeled into the center of the room. I can remember seeing the eyes of the couple light up when they saw my sister as she sat crumpled up in her wheelchair clasping her hands tight in a fist as she rocked back and forth. The lady grabbed her hands in hers and started sweetly talking to her, "God told me you are going to be healed. I am so excited for you. We are going to witness a miracle here!"

The couple then turned to us and said, "We have four tapes that have the book of John recorded on them. We believe that if you play these tapes in your daughter's room while she is sleeping and pray and fast for her for one month, by the end of that time Laura will be healed." My dad took the tapes and said, "We will try it. I have been praying for years for her, but if you think this will move God, I want nothing more than to see my daughter healed."

The lady looked very sternly at all of us, "But I must tell you, when you pray, you must pray believing or she will not be healed." My dad interrupted, "What do you mean by that?" The lady said in a more direct tone, "You must pray believing. That means if you drive out all of the doubt that is in your hearts and have a faith that is strong and pure, you can move mountains. Can you do that?" My dad said, "Sure, we will agree to pray. All of us will."

The couple left and gave final instructions, "Remember, play the tapes while she is sleeping and have everyone fast. We know God is going to do great things!" We watched the couple leave and get into their car. As they headed down the drive, I can remember a couple of my sisters asking, "Wow, that was weird. Dad, do you think Laura can actually be healed?"

"If it is the Lord's will, he can do anything he wants to. Wouldn't it be great to see Laura in her right mind and be able to live a normal life like the rest of us?" We all agreed, and he said, "So let's pray, fast one day a week, and if God wants to heal Laura, he will heal her!"

So, for the next month, my mom and dad played the John tapes as we prayed and fasted. I can remember wondering how to pray without having any doubt. I dreamed of what it would look like to see my sister completely healed, and I was getting excited about seeing God do a miraculous work. As the month went by, I saw absolutely no change in my sister's condition, she still needed to be fed, my mom continued to change her diapers, and she still drooled after drinking a glass of water.

Well, the month was over and it was time for the couple to come over to check on Laura's progress. The window for God's will was closing fast, and still, there was no sign of answered prayer. When the couple finally arrived, we once again gathered in the same room and wheeled Laura in the same way. The lady looked at Laura and then said to us, "Did you keep playing the tapes?" My dad nodded. "Did you fast all month?" My dad nodded again. "But someone must not have been praying believing." She turned to me and my sister, and said, "Did you both pray believing, because if you didn't it may have stopped the work of God."

My dad stood up and addressed the lady with a very imposing glare. I have seen him like this before and it was not good. He said, "Wait a minute, you cannot place blame on any of us for not praying with enough faith. That is a horrible burden of guilt you are placing on someone. God never works like that." The lady looked astonished, my mom chuckled because she knew not to mess with my dad when it came to Laura and defending his family.

"Well, we just want to see your daughter healed." Said the woman. I thought to myself, *Uh oh, she shouldn't have said that.* My dad was hot, "Don't you think I want to see my daughter healed? Don't you think I have gone to God and pleaded with him about her condition for years? Don't come in here with your false piety and thinking God hears you more than he hears my family.

Christianity is not magic. Nor is it a competition in holiness, it is trusting in the heart of God and knowing that his plans will always prevail."

He opened the front door and escorted the couple out. The husband said, "We just wanted you to experience the blessing of God like we have." My dad just ushered them out the door and said, "Have a good day." We never heard from them again. And to this day my sister is still not healed.

True faith is not grasping for miracles. It is being obedient even in the middle of darkness and confusion. Even after the couple left, my mom and dad never stopped praying for Laura, like they always had before. They also kept caring for her, like they always had before. They also expected us not to blame God for a world that seemed broken. They wanted us to trust him, knowing that heaven is our true home.

God may not answer our prayers in the immediate, but watching my dad with my sweet sister Laura I have learned that God has his reasons, and I should allow him those reasons. Genuine, powerful, life-altering faith says I will trust him forever until his wonderful kingdom comes. And it is there that all my dreams will finally come true.

---

* Some of the material in this chapter is taken from my book "My Silent Sister & Her Rusty Cage."

EIGHT:
Men at Work

"A person can do nothing better than to eat and
drink and find satisfaction in their own work.
This too, I see, is from the hand of God."
— *Ecclesiastes 2:24*

There are two kinds of football coaches in the world, Steve
Madden and everyone else.

Playing high school football was one of the greatest
highlights of my life. I miss the camaraderie I had with my
teammates. I miss the smell of newly cut grass on the football field
before practice in the middle of August. I love the touch, look, and
feel of a fresh new jersey the coach hands out to you before the first
game of the season. And then, of course, there is the big moment,
Friday Night Lights: the band, the fight song, the cheers, the
cheerleaders, the shine of the helmets, the rush of adrenaline, and
then the kickoff. Oh, the joy of being a modern-day gladiator!

But there is one thing I do not miss about football. It is
the reason I almost stopped playing the sport altogether. In fact, if
it was not for the grit of my dear mother who forced me to join the
team and face my fear head-on, I would not have played four full
years of High School ball. And that fear was the dreaded two-a-

day practices. If there was ever a foretaste of hell, two-a-day practices in the heat of a blazing August sun for a Bay Village high school football player was it. Talk about long days! The coaches would have you wake up with the early morning sun by arriving fully outfitted on the field at 6:00 a.m., and there you would practice until noon. The coaches allowed you to go home for lunch, and then you had to drag yourself back onto the field at 3:00 p.m. The misery would then last until 7:00 p.m. and you were so tired you would end up going right to bed the moment you got back home.

This went on for 14 long, grueling, murderous days. And coaches in the early eighties would hold back water breaks if the team was not practicing well. Coaches didn't connect proper hydration with peak performance as they do now. Two-a-days were like training in the Sahara Desert while running out of water in your canteen.

But the belly of the two-a-day beast was the dreaded giant sledding hill. In the center of Bay Village, Ohio there is a hill, and on that hill is grass, and on that grass in winter is snow. And on that snow go sleds and toboggans and inner-tubes and snowboards and even large cardboard refrigerator boxes. People from all over the neighborhood and surrounding suburbs would bring their families to enjoy the frozen slopes. "Zoom!" Down you would go all the way to the bottom. But in the middle of August people didn't go down that hill, oh no, the whole football team got to run up it during two-a-day practices.

I hated it! I mean, absolutely, utterly, completely hated it! The number of times the team would run up the hill all depended on how well practice for the day went. If it was a good day of practice, you only had to run up it five times. But if practice was a train wreck the team had to run ten or more. I heard the horror stories of running hills; some guys would spew out their guts, others would collapse halfway up, looking like a dead soldier that was shot on the Normandy beachhead during World War 2, and then you had the vast majority that would end up crawling to the top of the hill in pain.

My first experience with the sledding hill was after a very bad day of practice. I was walking with my fellow Freshman teammates toward the hill with the same trepidation and fear under a dark cloud of gloom. I imagined as if we were prisoners in a Russian work camp as they headed to break rocks at the limestone quarries of Siberia. As we approached the hill all the coaches stood on top while they pointed down to the very bottom telling us all to line up down there. There were about 100 players in all with the Seniors heading down to line up first. Every player could feel the dread hanging over them. I think some believed they were going to die.

The head coach at the top of the hill had his whistle in his hand while the seniors got ready to run on his signal. "Ready, set," *TWEEET* And the Seniors took off up the hill, immediately the big guys started falling behind while the lighter thinner guys glided up the hill huffing and puffing. A few of the largest players were already on their hands and knees crawling to the top. "Next group!" The coach yelled as the Juniors got ready. *TWEEET* They were off. And then the Sophomores lined up. *TWEEET* And they were off.

It was now the Freshman's turn—my group. Sweat was rolling down the center of my back before we even began. Right before the head coach was about to blow the whistle, Steve Madden, the Freshman coach, joined us on the line to run. "Okay guys," he said, "We can do this. Just follow my lead, one hill at a time and we will have no trouble with this." I was dumbfounded. Mr. Madden didn't have to enter hell with us, but he did, he ran with us and encouraged us up the hill for every run. Was it still hard? Yes, it was. Did some guys still throw up? Of Course! But with Mr. Madden running with us we knew we were going to survive, and it even became, dare I say it, enjoyable! After we ran a good seven hills we were done, most of us laying spread eagle on the grass at the top of the hill trying to catch our breath. And there was Mr. Madden, helping all of us up with a big smile on his face, saying, "See, I told you we could do it!" And we did. And then he said, "Doesn't it feel great to get stronger—no pain, no gain!"

And when it comes to approaching work and teaching your sons and daughters about tackling a career, there are two kinds of fathers—those who point the stern finger of a hard disciplinarian who stands on top of the hill yelling and insisting, and then you have the Steve Madden type of dad who portrays work as both enjoyable and a great gift given to us from God.

Most dads never seem satisfied with the choices of their children and think anger and constant disappointment is how you teach your son to work hard and "make a name for themselves." Work is not meant to be fun, it is a human being's lot in life—to grunt and grind under thorns and thistles, to run up the hills of misery, puking your guts out. So, work for most of us has become nothing more than a curse word, something to hold your nose while doing it, trying to hang on as long as you can until you retire.

And then you have fathers like Steve Madden, they fully jump in with you in the mud, dirt, grease, sawdust, cow manure, wet cement, smelly mulch, and constant sweat of work, teaching and encouraging you all along the way. My dad was like Mr. Madden. He lifted the concept of work out of the despised pit and brought it up to be something that can be a lifelong adventure, and yes, it can even be enjoyable. He was with me, not playing the role of judge, or arrogant construction foreman who saw menial labor as below his station, or even a white-collar paper pusher stuck in his office away from the regular rabble, but my dad was always happy to be seen as a fellow co-laborer.

3 E's OF WORK

When your dad works alongside you, you naturally learn from his example. I remember digging holes and carrying wood with my dad, watching every move he made. I was always impressed when I would watch how his massive forearms could wield a hammer, or he was very intent on showing me how to properly lift a wheelbarrow without tipping over the mixed concrete. He stood next to me to show me how to hold a shovel or grease a bicycle wheel while sitting on the driveway next to my brother and me. Sometimes while we would work, he wouldn't say a word, other times he would tell me how certain skills would improve my future. Through watching and listening to him, I learned that work required three things: A good ethic, skilled expertise, and of course, enjoyment. If you didn't like what you were doing you would eventually stop doing it.

LESSON ONE: Work Ethic

"Chris," my dad would say, "people will pay big money for a person they can trust. Skills and abilities can be taught, but an employee that will bust their butt even when the boss is gone will always find work." This mattered more to him than anything. He hated it when I would complain about calluses or whine about the heat. He believed a man was designed by God to work and when he worked hard there was a deep satisfaction you could achieve no other way. So for him to work, to sweat, to build, to make, to clean, and even simply having a job was an incredible privilege. Some of this was learned through his father's fear of not having a job growing up during the Great Depression, but mostly it was from knowing he was responsible to provide for his family and teach his sons how to be providers as well. "Chris", he would insist, "when you are employed you need to learn to shut your mouth because you have a job and you are making money. That is something to be proud of."

Good work ethic is all about the character of a person. And character matters more than momentary success or even the size of your paycheck. Character, in the end, will always be rewarded and it is easy to acquire. You don't need a diploma or degree to have good character, you don't even need to prove you are better than others in the office or job site. You simply need to show up on time and do what you are told. These two things are sadly lacking in employees these days. And if the job is hard, just remember, "no pain, no gain."

One of the most important lessons my dad insisted on when it came to "work ethic" was the concept of "making them miss you" when you are gone. Rare is the person that is wanted, being a breath of fresh air when they enter a building. Bringing a burst of sunshine in the office takes real effort and you need to be intentional about it. My dad insisted you come to work to serve others and be there to make other people's day. Don't be the employee who demands his own way or is never satisfied. Too often people act like they are God's gift to the office, they deserve special treatment just for showing up, or some even expect a pay raise every other month. That kind of attitude drove my dad crazy. "Be a blessing", was his motto.

So I tried to do this. One of the first jobs I got out of college was working for a large well-known company in Cleveland.

There was a man there named Jimmy. Jimmy was a custodian. He did mundane work like mopping the floors, cleaning the bathrooms, taking out everyone's garbage, and making sure all general maintenance was taken care of. Jimmy was a hard worker, but no one paid him much attention. I told my dad about Jimmy and he said that Jimmy was an important person too, so to make his job a joy.

I got to know Jimmy and I asked him every day about his family, assisted him when he needed some help moving a heavy desk, and just acknowledged him as a living being made in God's image. I will never forget the day I left for another job. Jimmy ran up to me as I was packing my office and said, "Mr. Weeks, I am sorry to see you go. Mr. Weeks, every day's a holiday when I see you. It is like the Fourth of July when I see your face. It is like Christmas Eve when I shake your hand. Every day's a holiday when I see Mr. Weeks!"

My dad was right. When you are a blessing people will miss you when you are gone.

LESSON TWO: Develop Expertise

A person never arrives, they always have something new to learn. Pride is the biggest problem with most employees. They think they know enough once they land a job, so they quit learning. And when you quit learning, you stop growing. Expertise and becoming excellent at what you do is always a work in progress. An object in motion must stay in motion, so it is with excellence and expertise. But growth requires a desire to grow and once you stop the progress, the opposite is also true. An object at rest stays at rest.

My dad was always willing to learn and each day offered new opportunities to grow. Whatever product he was selling, he learned all he could about it. Every new person he met was also an opportunity to learn more. Most people look down on others, thinking they are better. My dad learned from others, letting them be the experts. When a person would come over to our house, he wanted us to first listen to them before we talked about ourselves. If a man was a carpenter, don't tell him how good you are at building but rather learn from him. If a lady is a writer, ask her for some of the tricks of her trade. Listen and learn.

When I became a pastor, I soon realized how people do not naturally do this. Even though I have been working in the church for over 25 years, people will instantly tell me how to pastor, give me tips on how to preach, and even how a pastor is just in it for the money. I know people mean well, but it does show they don't realize who they are talking to.

Expertise requires a constant internal drive to become really good at what you do. Never be satisfied. If you need more schooling to be better, get it. If you have to find someone who can teach you to be better, ask them to show you. Learn all that you can while you can, and you will make yourself both a respected and indispensable employee. A favorite verse for my dad was Proverbs

22:29, "Do you see someone skilled in their work? They will serve before kings; they will not serve before officials of low rank."

As a salesman, my dad always worked on his closing techniques. He would try different methods he read in books or learned at sales seminars. He would talk to us at home about some of the methods of getting people to buy. I remember when he told us, "The first thing you need to learn about a close is once you make the offer, the first person to speak loses." My brother learned this so well he once made a deal over the phone to a customer after waiting for 20 minutes in silence. Apparently, the man on the other side also knew the same trick so they were both waiting for the other person to speak first.

My dad learned his products so well that over time he knew how they worked better than the manufacturer who made them. That is why he brought home the microwaves and refrigerators with the ice cream makers that he sold. He wanted to believe in the product so he could be honest when he sold them. And then when he met his customers, he made sure to make a lasting impression on them. They were not going to forget Don Weeks, if he could help it.

To help accomplish this, his favorite thing to do was to have my mom make him crazy ties. He would go to the fabric store and pick out the nuttiest material he could find for her to make ties. From juggling clowns to yellow smiley faces, he would go the extra mile just to make a difference. Then he would show up at large appliance dealerships wearing his ties and introduce himself to everyone. It takes a lot of courage to be yourself, even to the point of embarrassment, but my dad was secure enough in who he was that he didn't mind being laughed at and considered a bit odd. One thing I could say for sure, he always left an unforgettable impression wherever he went. People couldn't forget my dad.

LESSON THREE: Enjoy Your Work

My dad loved movies, and especially on slow Saturdays when the weather was bad we would get some peanuts and popcorn, hunker down in the living room, and watch some of his old favorites together. There was nothing like watching movies with my dad. We wouldn't just sit there; we would talk about the themes and comment on the actors. Movies were a platform for discussion and developing a philosophy for living rather than wasting a mere day to be slavishly entertained.

He especially loved the movie Cool Hand Luke. Luke, the main protagonist, was a petty criminal who was imprisoned for two years at a prison farm where the warden was cruel and uncompromising. The men at the prison camp loved Luke because he refused to cave into the pressure of conforming to the warden's iron rule.

The scene my dad liked the most was when the prisoners were formed into a road crew where they had to throw sand over hot tar being spread on the local highway. It was in the middle of summer in the south, and the air was humid and thick. It reminded me of a two-a-day practice in Bay Village. The men were dreading the job they were tasked to do so they lumbered slowly out of the prison truck to grudgingly pick up their shovels. Luke would not give into the mob's mentality, instead, he decided to see how fast they could get this horrible job done.

With a smile and a buoyant spirit, he inspired the rest of the prisoners to attack the job with zeal. He would attack each pile of sand with joy. At first, his fellow prisoners thought he was a madman, but soon they all started smiling and running to see how fast they could get the job done. The prison bosses didn't like it because they wanted the men to be miserable. Instead, they realized with Luke around they could find purposeful living even working on a prison chain gang.

"Chris, do you see that?" My Dad's eyes would shine, "Do you see how you don't have to let circumstances form your attitude? You decide if your job is going to be an adventure or a drudgery. Most people see work as a burden, but it isn't! Work is a gift, so attack whatever your hands find to do with gusto."

Another movie he raved about was A Christmas Carol. He brought to our attention the scene where Mr. Fezziwig, Ebenezer Scrooge's first boss, would have dancing parties for his employees. "Even old Scrooge remembered those days with fondness." He pointed out. And of course he loved the part when Ebenezer transformed at the end of the story—the classic scene after Scrooge changed his disposition then tried going back to work in his office but couldn't stop laughing for having another chance at life. And in his joy, he threw his feathered quill in the air and said, "I don't deserve to be this happy."

"That's it! Right there," my dad would point out, "There's the truth. No one deserves anything, and because of God's grace, we have been given another chance to live. So live it! Work with joy. And don't expect anything from anybody. You want something, earn it." As John F. Kennedy once said, "Ask not what your country can do for you, but ask what you can do for your country.

I once read a book written by a man who interviewed over a hundred people who were facing a terminal illness and were about to die. The interviewer wanted to highlight what were the most important insights people had before they breathed their last. One of his concluding observations described my dad to a tee, "Not one of the people who were dying ever wished they worked more. Most of them wished they could have found a job that they enjoyed and one that also gave them enough money to have the freedom to spend their time with their family and friends. Life is about living, not working." This is a delicate balance and my dad found this. When he died, he was not considered rich in monetary terms, nor in the capital he acquired, but he did leave countless memories with his family. He was a great provider, but an even better friend and father.

NINE:
A Lover of Music

"Is anyone among you suffering? Let him pray.
Is anyone cheerful? Let him sing praise."
— *James 5:13*

A sardine can couldn't have been packed any tighter. The Week's family station wagon was stuffed to the gills as we headed down the Pennsylvania Turnpike towards our summer vacation rental cottage to spend a whole week in Virginia Beach. My dad packed his family of eight tight, including all of our clothes, a week's worth of food, and my sister's friend Janey even joined us for the eleven-hour leisurely road trip to the Atlantic coast. My dad loved driving, and he especially enjoyed taking his time cruising through the mountains marveling at all the scenery. When he was away from work on vacation, he tried to make time with his family last as long as possible. But for us kids, the drive was torture; I had to sit next to my sweaty sisters as they picked their gnarly toenails. Talk about uncomfortable, we were dying in that car. And the worst part of all was my mom only had a large green thermos full of her black Maxwell House coffee for us to drink. Sometimes I was so famished I relented and took a couple of sips.

I think that is where I began my addiction with only drinking straight black roast.

Halfway through the trip the moaning and groaning couldn't be contained anymore. "Dad, how much longer do we have?" "Dad, it's so hot in this car." "Dad, Laura is slobbering on my pants." He had enough. "Okay, okay, you guys. Here is what we are going to do." But instead of pulling the car over and slapping us silly, he chose a better way to calm his brood of savage beasts. His solution was to sing. "All right, join with me..."

I've got ten pence, jolly, jolly ten pence,
I've got ten pence, to last me all my life:
I've got five pence to spend, and five pence to lend,
But no pence to give back to my wife, poor wife...

On and on the song went. At first we did not want to smile, because let's face it, it's easier to complain. But after a minute or so, his singing overpowered the mood in the car where the whole bunch of us forgot the distress of our long drive and we were belting out my dad's old favorite sing-a-longs at the top of our voices. We sang songs like *100 Bottles of Beer on the Wall* and Don Ho's classic, *Tiny Bubbles.*

Because my dad sang all the time, we knew these songs by heart, and soon the misery of being cooped up in our jail on wheels faded away. Looking back on those long car rides, it turned out that they provided some of the best memories I ever had as a kid.

The gray grumble cloud was lifted and we rode in the joy of the melody as it carried us along: *"Country Roads, take me home, to the place, I belong...,"* on and on it went. Laughter and song proved themselves to have superior power over the moaning and groaning of mob disquiet. Music flowed easily off the lips of my dad, and I cannot remember a day going by without him breaking out in a popular song or melody to brighten up the atmosphere.

A WAY OF LIFE

When I think back to what it was like growing up in our house, music was a huge part of surviving through mundane human tedium. Both my mom and dad always had some sort of record player on, a mixed tape playing on a boom box, or the old AM/FM radio in the garage belting out classics that my dad would more than likely be singing along with. *"Trailers for sale or rent, rooms let for 50 cents..."* Or, *"Raindrops keep falling on my head..."* Singing was as normal to us as the sun rising, but now that I look back on growing up as Don Weeks' son, I realize how rare it was to have a dad who sings.

He sang all the time. As a child, my dad grew up in a home with a mom who loved opera and always banged out simple marches and classics on their old upright piano. It formed in my father a deep love for music. He never received any professional training, melody just flowed out from the core of his being. He was born with rhythm and jive. He was also born with the looks and talent of a dark-haired Italian crooner who was blessed with a deep melodic voice to match. He would often joke, "I once sang on the television," and then he would grin, "but my mom told me to get off—I was scratching the set."

During Christmas time he played Sinatra and Johnny Mathis records. Summer was full of Beach Boy tunes and of course the classic "Lazy, Crazy, Hazy Days of Summer." Every occasion had a song. Whatever he heard, he sang. It could be a little advertisement ditty about the Roto-Rooter plumber in town or a new Jimmy Buffet song about "Margaritaville." He didn't care what the song was, if it had a catchy tune, he sang it.

Dean Martin and the fifties crooners were his very favorite. Sometimes when we would be sitting around the dinner table eating my mom's spaghetti and meatball meal, he would break out with, *"When... the... moon hits your eye like a big pizza pie, that's Amore'"* while rolling a fork full of pasta on his spoon. Another classic memory on many a lazy Saturday night was when my dad would put on a record like Jose Feliciano's, "Light My Fire" and lie down on his back in the middle of the living room and just listen to it.

Musicals on television also seemed to always be on in our home during the weekend afternoons, generating an atmosphere of song that permeated our house. *Mary Poppins, Wizard of Oz, Singin' in the Rain, Grease,* and of course, *The Music Man* were some of our old favorites. Singing was never simply to be enjoyed by girly girls and artistic sensitive males, I was raised knowing that it was meant for all of us to express the joy and sorrow of life, even rugged men like my dad.

My sisters and I constantly put on musical plays for my mom and dad to watch, with *The Sound of Music* being the main performance. To this day I know every song from the Rodgers and Hammerstein masterpiece, and I am not ashamed to admit it. When it was time for "Edelweiss" to be sung my dad couldn't sit still, he had to get up and lead it with all of us, his voice range was a perfect fit. And I also think he liked to consider himself kindred spirit with Captain von Trapp, a strong man, with a big family and a velvety smooth voice.

THE GIFT OF WORSHIP

It was clear he loved music in general—I will not use the word "secular music" because music is music and if sung well for the purpose of edifying others or expressing delight, there is a grace-filled quality about it. But the one thing my dad relished more than anything else was praising his God. When the church was gathered to worship, he wanted to be a part of it. He truly delighted in telling his God how much he loved him in song. "Chris," he would say with genuine enthusiasm, "listen to the lyrics of this song!" And then he would put on a tape of Phil Driscoll, the fabulous trumpeter, while belting out the lyrics to "I Exalt Thee"...

For Thou, o Lord, art high above all the earth
Thou art exalted far above all gods
For Thou, o Lord, art high above all the earth
Thou art exalted far above all gods
I exalt Thee, I exalt Thee
I exalt Thee, o Lord
I exalt Thee, I exalt Thee
I exalt Thee, o Lord

Every church he was a part of, if they had a choir, he joined it. He sang in numerous Christmas cantatas and joined special Easter praise teams. He even was part of the Billy Graham 10,000 voice choir during the 1994 crusade in his hometown of Cleveland. He didn't care if the music was composed of old hymns, Gregorian chants, or new 7/11 praise choruses, if there was an opportunity to lift your voice to Jesus, he wanted to join in.

Even sitting in a pew next to my dad in church, I could always count on him to freely sing out. There was no reason to be embarrassed. God was the main audience, so no one else really mattered. In fact, one unfortunate consequence of my dad's incessant singing is that he would often lose his voice in the middle of December right when the choir had a Christmas concert planned, but he still went in front of the church in his choir robe and gave it his all for God even if no sound came out.

I will never forget when the song *In Christ Alone* first became popular in churches. There was something about that song that struck a deep chord with my dad. It spoke to him as much as a good sermon did. He was more excited about singing that song at Sunday service than he would be about watching his favorite sports team or movie later that afternoon. This song perfectly expressed what he was living for, and what life meant to him. Worshipping Christ and Christ alone! During the memorial service for my dad, my mom made sure it was one of the songs we sang together as a family. And the church he was an elder at put the lyrics to *In Christ Alone* on a nice, formatted picture frame that is still hanging in the church's hallway in commemoration of my dad, Elder Don Weeks. Music spoke to my dad because he let it in.

Some of the readers might be wondering why I am including a chapter on music as an important ingredient to being a good dad. It is because music adds tremendous value to life, it infuses joy and meaning to the mundane parts of the day. It reflects a world that is ruled by a happy God. And it breathes hope into a weary soul. In the same way our complaining stopped once we started singing in a sweaty station wagon, when music and song become a regular part of living it makes the heaviness of life lighter. This is something people have forgotten. No one sings as a family anymore, instead, we sit on couches staring at electronics while we watch others sing to us. We have moved from participants to lethargic consumers, and that is not a good thing.

But when a family sings together, it naturally unites their hearts. Try not to feel community and a smile welling up in your chest when everyone is blasting out the chorus to Sweet Caroline,

"Sweet Caroline, bum-bum-bum, good times never seemed so good!" Singing music may sound like a trivial matter to most, but it wasn't to my dad. It was a way he communicated a real zest for living, he felt fortunate to be alive and when he sang you could tell.

I can remember a Saturday afternoon when my dad came home and most of my family was sitting around the living room just talking about nothing. He said, "Hey, there is a new polka pizza joint that just opened up a few blocks away. Who wants to go?" We weren't doing anything, and my dad seemed really excited about it, so most of us kids and my mom went.

When we walked in, there was an organ and a large man with a chubby red face singing songs over a microphone while he was aggressively hammering down on the keys of his large organ. About a dozen or so people were sitting at cheap-looking tables eating pizza and swilling beer. And then our large family walked in and our group almost doubled the size of the whole place. While we were ordering, the man behind the microphone asked if anybody had any special song requests. My dad said, "Do you know *Roll Out the Barrel?*"

"Of course I do!" The man replied and turned up the volume, alone with the cheesy polka reverb on the organ. He then led the whole place in a raucous sing along of the old Polish favorite: *"Roll out the barrel, we'll have a barrel of fun..."* I never thought eating cheap cardboard pizza and drinking Coca-Cola out of red plastic cups could be so much fun! Music has a way of bringing the world together.

THAT'S AMORE'

I would like to share a final story that will put a bow on the gift given to us called music. My sister Gina was turning 40 and so her husband Mike wanted to do something special to surprise her. Mike thrives on spontaneity mixed with a big tablespoon of craziness and his plan to surprise my sister included both in heavy measure. I was sitting in my office at work in Michigan when I received a call on my cell phone, "Hey Christo Magico, this is your brother-in-law, Mike." Of course, it was Mike. No one else in the world calls me Christo Magico but him.

"Hey, I have a great idea to surprise Gina for her 40th, but it will require you to fly down to California for a couple of days." I caught my breath and replied, "You want me to fly down to California for a couple of days? Mike, her birthday is only a few weeks away!"

"Chris, don't worry about the details. I have a boatload of frequent flyer miles and flights are cheap right now. All you need to do is agree to come and I will figure out the rest." Mike also happens to be a very successful financial advisor, so his persuasive abilities are second to none. "Okay Mike," I relented, "What is the plan?"

A few weeks later I jumped on a cheap Southwestern red-eye flight to Los Angeles and his son, Marc, was waiting at the airport to pick me up. He then drove me to a fancy Italian restaurant near their house and gave me a crazy outfit to put on. It included a big white chef's hat, a large black Mario-looking mustache, and a white apron padded in the belly to make me look like a fat Italian man.

"Okay Uncle Chris," my nephew said, "This is a singing restaurant and when my family comes in, we will get a big table. After we order my dad wants you to come out holding a plate of spaghetti singing *That's Amore* by Dean Martin. Just sing it as loud as you can while walking toward the table. Make sense?"

Having flown out just for this occasion, I had no other choice, so I said, "Let's do this!" He told me he had to go home and that they would arrive at the restaurant in a couple of hours. So, there I sat waiting to surprise my sister. Sure enough, a short time later two large SUVs pulled up to the restaurant. Piling out was my sister's whole family, which included her three kids, their friends, her in-laws, and even my mom and dad. *What is my dad doing here?* I wondered, as I went to the backroom to hide while my sister's family was escorted by a blond-haired hostess to the table they reserved.

I eventually saw my brother-in-law Mike get up from the table, probably telling everyone he had to use the restroom. When he came to the back room where I was, he was adorning a mile-wide grin and hugged me. "Chris, this is going to be great! Thanks for coming, Gina has no idea you are here, neither does your mom and dad."

"Okay Mike," I said, "When do you want me to come out?"

"We will order, and the main waiter will tell you when the spaghetti is ready and will give you a plate to bring out. Hold it high in your right hand and start singing as loud as you can. Got it?"

"I've got it!"

Looking at my costume, Mike punched me in my padded belly and said, "You look perfect. I am so excited about this!"

I could see them all ordering and then they gave the waiter the menus. I could feel a kaleidoscope of butterflies doing flips in my stomach as I waited to surprise my family while embarrassing myself at the same time. A dark-haired waiter approached me trying to force down a chuckle when he saw my silly outfit. Handing me a plate full of spaghetti he said, "Are you ready? It is time." I nodded, took a huge breath, and started walking slowly through the restaurant.

When I was a few tables away I began to sing at the top of my lungs really exaggerating the syllables, *"W-h-h-e-e-n-n….the moon hits your eye like a big pizza pie, that's amore'. When the stars seem to shine like you've had too much wine, that's amore'…"*

My sister stood up instantly and stared. Dropping her fork of pasta, she started walking slowly toward me, "Wait, wait, I know that voice!" She looked at me and exclaimed, "What in the world?!? Chris, what are you doing here?" Smiling, crying, laughing, and punching her husband Mike, she said, "Chris, this is incredible. I couldn't ask for a better present!" She ran over and gave me a giant hug, almost knocking over the plate of spaghetti I was holding in my hand. All the while this was going on my dad turned, looked toward me with a puzzled expression, and said, "Why is Gina hugging that strange-looking Italian man?"

I replied, "Dad, it's me, Chris!" He still didn't understand. So I took off my mustache and hat and he said, "Chris, I didn't know you worked in California. When did you move here?" Mike tried to explain the whole story to him, but he still wasn't tracking. So, I asked him, "Didn't you recognize the song and my voice when I was walking toward you? I tried to sing it just like you!"

He replied without missing a beat, "It was pretty good, but I thought that a restaurant this fancy could find a little bit better singer." He then laughed out loud, gave me a hug, and said, "I want to eat, I am starving!" Oh, the power of music and how it knits hearts together. I wonder what Jesus' voice sounds like.

TEN:
Apples of Gold

"Listen, my sons, to a father's instruction;
pay attention and gain understanding."
— *Proverbs 4:1*

Words have power! Even though they are merely sounds that contain small units of meaning traveling through the air from one person to another, their capacity to effect change in the life of another can never be taken for granted. Even if the old adage claims that "sticks and stones may break my bones, but words will never hurt me", the reality, according to scripture, is that words categorically do hurt, and more importantly, they can also bless.

As Proverbs 18:21 puts it, "the tongue has the power of life and death." Especially words from a father. They have the potential to destroy a child or build them up; they can emotionally scar a boy and girl for life or fuel a son's soul with courage and a daughter's dreams for success. I believe God designed a dad's words to land heavy as a ton of lead on the heart of his child. One word from a dad has the potential to change a life, while a hundred from a teacher and a thousand from a preacher barely penetrates the thick exterior of the mind. So, when dad speaks, like an ice pick to the brain, the words are sure to pierce. So, dad, take heed, whenever you speak, the stakes are always high.

When God the Father wanted to communicate to the children of the world, he sent his Son. Jesus translated the glorious and transcendent language of heaven into human flesh. That is why he is known as the "Word" or "Logos", through him God was talking directly to us in our own language. And when he spoke, those listening noticed that all of his words had "authority" and a power that came straight from the Father himself. As Jesus said, "I have not spoken on my own, but the Father who sent me has commanded me to say all that I have spoken." When we listen to Jesus, we hear the direct words that God the Father wanted us to hear. And those words were and are always pregnant with life. John said when Jesus spoke, his words were full of both "grace" and "truth." He spoke kindly and he always spoke what actually is.

That is a human father's job as well—to tell the truth to his children while saturating those words with kindness. Fathers must speak what reality is like, but it must also be done in a way that communicates grace. This is an enormous task. Sadly, many a father has relinquished this job and spoken to their children with only words of harshness and folly. Some dads don't even speak up at all. The silent strong type of man may sound like a good character in a movie, John Wayne standing tall at the Alamo or Arnold Schwarzenegger chomping on a cigar getting into a Hummer, but these types of men make for a cold uncaring world in real-time. Maybe that is why we have a crisis of faith in our churches. Natural fathers don't take seriously enough the power they have been given and as a result, the image of God has been marred and distorted.

An experience I had as a youth pastor is a vivid example of how much power a father can wield in his child's life. A 9th-grade boy came into my office to see me and he was trembling with fear as he started to share what was on his heart. "Pastor Chris, I really do not know what to do."

"What's up?" I said in a nonchalant way to try to keep the tension level down. I could tell he was terribly scared and nervous to tell me what was happening in his life.

"Well, my dad is coming in to talk with you and he is super-duper mad. Last week I got my hair dyed red for spirit week and he wants to kick me out of the house because he said I looked like a girl."

"He wants to kick you out for that?" It sounded ridiculous.

"He keeps saying something about how only girls dye their hair. So I tried to explain to him how most of the guys in the school colored their hair red, but he wouldn't listen and sent me to my room. He said he is coming in to talk to you so you can address how boys should not dress like girls." He dropped his head and added, "I'm sorry, he will be here after youth group."

As I was teaching up on stage during youth group, I noticed a rather tall and heavyset man with a thick black beard standing in the corner with his arms crossed and a furrowed brow, focused straight on me. I knew right away this was the boy's dad who was waiting to talk. I could see the son slinking down in his chair, trying not to be noticed. When youth group was over, I immediately went over to the dad and invited him into my office. He did not look happy. But I thanked him for coming in and asked how I could help him.

"Well, I'm sure my son already talked to you and told you what a horrible father I am, but I've come in because I think you have a lot of influence over him. We have hired you to teach our kids correct behavior and some of his decisions have me really worried as of late. I know the Bible talks about how a man must not dress like a woman, and because of that, I will not stand for my son dying his hair like some silly teenage girl would. I need to draw the line in my family and I need you to support me on this."

You could see the fire in his eyes, and also it was obvious that he was accustomed to using his size and deep voice to intimidate people into doing what he wanted. I could only imagine what it would be like growing up in this man's house and my heart instantly went out for his son.

Instead of backing down to his demand, I decided to confront him. I realized that he needed to answer a couple of questions for me first, "Sir, do you know what spirit week is at the High School?" He shook his head no, so I continued, "Well, it is a way for the whole school to encourage the football team to win the game and show your school spirit. It has nothing to do with being a transgender or homosexual, but it is simply an innocent and fun way of showing support for your team." He kept his arms crossed and the furrow on his brow deepened. I continued, "So is it okay with you to possibly lose your son over an issue that I, personally, don't think is even on God's radar?"

You could see he was not liking being on the other side of direct questioning. He wasn't used to it. He looked at me and said, "Women dye their hair. The Bible says men should not dress like women. Therefore, if my son has dyed his hair red he must be sinning. And I think you need to back me up on this."

I have developed a philosophy when I minister, especially when it comes to people in the church who demand you to do their bidding, I will not take responsibility for something that is not mine to take. But I also will not back down when I think a person is acting selfish or being unreasonable. Clearly, this father did not understand the intent of scripture nor did he even care to listen to the perspective of his son. So, I replied, "Sir, if you keep harping on this tiny issue, you are going to lose your son. You also do not understand how to properly assess scripture. By missing the context of the command, you are also missing the principal God intended altogether. Give your son some grace, it really is not that big a deal."

His angry eyes flashed hot and immediately the dad got up and said, "We are done with this church and I am not allowing my son to come back here and be taught by such a feminized youth pastor like you." Huffing out of my office the dad turned to his son who was sitting in the hallway, the boy's head was buried under his hands, and he said to him, "Get up and let's get out of this liberal church!"

As the angry bull of a man steamed past his son, the boy looked at me with tear-filled eyes and slumped shoulders. He was crushed under the weight of his dad's unwillingness to budge on his opinion. He slowly slinked down the church hallway and out the door. I never saw the sad boy again.

SPEAKING GRACE

Yup, words have power! And my dad knew how to use that power. I thank God he did, he knew when to apply grace and he also knew when to tell the truth. And because of his understanding of how to maintain this delicate balance, I am a blessed man for it. Scripture is very clear on this in Ephesians 6:4, "Fathers, do not exasperate your children; instead, bring them up in the training and instruction of the Lord." The key phrase is "not to exasperate." Exasperation is when these concepts are either out of skew or missing altogether but when the blend is balanced and both ingredients are present, that is when words have positive effects.

As I said earlier, grace includes kindness, and kindness presumes that careful understanding went into the words before they escaped the mouth. One of the greatest conversations I had with my dad when it came to using words of grace was during a casual game of H.O.R.S.E. He had just come home from work and we were playing on the driveway and in between shooting the basketball my dad decided to strike up a conversation. "Chris, how was school today, you look a little down?"

I answered as I usually would, "I'm fine dad. Nothing really happened, just another boring day in class." I dribbled and missed a short shot. He said, "Chris, I'm not stupid, I can tell something is really bothering you. What is it?" I was hesitant to tell him what happened earlier that day on the playground at recess, so I evaded. "It's nothing."

"It's not nothing, Chris, you are not usually so down in the dumps. What's going on? I'm your dad, give me the low down." He said as he swished a nice ten-foot shot in the corner.

Dribbling to the spot he just made it from I sheepishly replied, "Well, some of the guys wonder why I won't talk to some of the popular girls who like me." I took the shot and made it.

"Nice shot," My dad said, and he continued, "So, why won't you talk to them?"

"I don't know what to say. My words are always so jumbled, and then…" He dribbled over to the top of the key and missed his shot.

"And then, what?" My dad wouldn't let up. I said nothing, so he asked again, "and then what? What happened after that?"

"Well, one of my friends wondered if I didn't like girls. He said maybe I liked guys better, and then he laughed at me." I took a long shot on the other side of the court because I felt a bit embarrassed about what I said. I made it.

"Who was the guy? Was it one of those loudmouthed Italian kids in class? Because I know a few of them are already shaving in the 7ᵗʰ grade and they get a little cocky." My dad took the ball to where I just shot it and he made it...*SWISH...nothing but net!*

"Well, yeah, it's one of the bigger guys that keeps bugging me. He thinks it's funny to make fun of how shy I am," I said. "But dad, I do wonder why I'm so small compared to some of those guys. And I don't feel as confident as they do. So maybe they're right because it sure is a lot easier for me to talk to my male friends."

My dad smiled and threw me the ball, "Chris, it's always easier to talk to your male friends at that age. Pretty girls are intimidating especially when you're a late bloomer." I took another shot but missed it.

"Late bloomer? What does that mean?"

"I was a late bloomer. During grade school I was shorter than most of the guys in my grade. They were all Italian and Irish. Italians and Irish have quick growth spurts so by the 8ᵗʰ grade most of them reach their adult height. But we are mutts, we have all kinds of nationalities in us, and mutts take some time to hit their growth spurt." He made a fancy hook shot from the right side off the key.

"So did you have a tough time talking to girls too?" I asked with a warm feeling rising in my gut. I tried the same hook shot but wildly missed.

"That is H-O for you, Chris. And yes, absolutely, I had a terrible time talking to girls. I would even blush when the pretty ones sat next to me in class. But the summer right before my Junior year in High School I sprouted up like a bad weed and grew taller than every Italian and Irish guy in my class. Not only that, but I also gained some heavy muscle as well as a newfound confidence. Asking girls out became easy because they started blushing around me." My dad made an easy layup with his left hand.

"Really? You grew taller than all of them?" I was starting to smile thinking about what he just said, and I made the layup with no problem at all.

"Yeah, I can remember it was also around my junior year when I began going to dances. We would do the jitterbug and I would do the slide move with girls where you slide them between your legs and sometimes, I would leave them sliding and walk off the dance floor." He laughed and missed a hook shot from the left side.

"Dad, c'mon, you didn't really do that, did you?" I asked making a tough shot from above the arc of the key.

"Nice shot! And yes, I did that! Chris, you need to realize that there's a time for everything. People these days want to push things, especially dating and sex, way, way too fast. Don't worry, you'll grow into your body. So enjoy the life you've been given, hang out with your friends, and play basketball with your dear old dad in the backyard while you can. And please Chris, don't grow up too fast. Life is flying by as it is." He missed the shot.

"That is H-O for you too, dad! I'm going to beat you this round dad." I felt like a million dollars.

"Remember, not so fast my boy. You have a long way to go before you beat me!" Winking at me, he drilled another right-handed hook shot. But I didn't care. It felt the world was taken off my shoulders, because of the grace of his words, and the way he could speak into my heart, he made me realize that I was going to be okay. I was normal for feeling this way.

My dad loved me, and his words proved it. Not only did he reassure me that my problems were not unique to me, but that the world didn't need to push me to places that were not healthy or even true. I thank God my dad protected me from the lies of an evil world that loves to prey on the fears and anxiety of the young. I am convinced the over-sexualization of our boys and girls is because dads are not there to speak grace into their children's hearts. They have quit being the protector and nurturer that God designed them to be.

Speaking grace means to first listen to your children with kindness and compassion and then answer them in a way that respects the dignity of that person. Instead of judgment and condemnation, grace allows for mistakes and even human failure, confusion, and questioning while using level-headed reason to calmly settle the waters of a worried soul. Grace seeks to teach by gentleness, not strong-arming your child's mind through intimidation and forced submission. You want a child who respects your words, not cringes every time they hear them.

SPEAKING TRUTH

Being a dad also means that the buck stops with you. This is where speaking the hard truth comes in. Truth does not budge; it is rock solid and hard-edged. At times a dad will be called on to tell it as it is. If he doesn't, then a child will be left to wander aimlessly in a seemingly meaningless world. Truth exists because God exists, and a dad has a responsibility to communicate the truth about God's existence.

We live in a world where parents are told to let their children figure things out for themselves. We encourage them to question everything, keep their options open, and not let rigid rules destroy their curiosity and inquisitiveness. All of that sounds well and good, that is until the granite wall of truth smacks your children hard in the face. And it will, because there is a real reality that God has made, with real standards, actual principles, warnings, and living promises that have rewards and curses attached to them. A good father needs to both know them and then teach them. If you don't, your child will be lost. And I am convinced you will someday have to answer for your disdainful neglect before the judgment seat of Jesus Christ himself.

One of the finest sounding lies people in the church have been suckered into believing is that you don't need to teach your child about God. They can figure out whether or not he exists on their own. So we are coolly told to let them explore on their own which religion is true. It sounds so reasonable and sophisticated, but I ask you, if something is true, isn't it true for everyone regardless of what they believe? So if God is true, fathers are responsible to teach the truth of his existence.

Think of it like this: what responsible parent would ever tell their children that they can figure out basic mathematics on their own? Who knows if 2 + 2 really equals 4? If your son or daughter wants it to be 5, is it up to them to decide? Should they be allowed to choose their own truth? Absolutely not! A good parent insists that the answer is 4 every time. And life will always bear this out. Something isn't true simply because a person chooses to believe it is true, it is true because it is based in reality.

Accordingly, everything God says in his Word is true. He speaks honestly about the way reality truly is. That is why Paul says in Galatians 6:7-8, "Do not be deceived: God cannot be mocked. A man reaps what he sows. Whoever sows to please their flesh, from the flesh will reap destruction; whoever sows to please the Spirit, from the Spirit will reap eternal life." So, dad, it is your responsibility to make sure your child grows up on the right side of the reaping.

My dad would often warn me with his words. When I needed a good hard rebuke, he wasn't scared of letting me have it. When I was getting a little too big for my britches, he would confront me with difficult questions and not be overly impressed with me just because I was his son. He also knew how to challenge me to be a better man. Here is one example of such a time. For seven years I was working as a youth pastor at our church. At the time I had four young kids at home and youth ministry required me to spend a large portion of that time out of the house. I would go on campouts, mission trips, and weeklong retreats with Junior and Senior High students. It was both fun and a tremendous opportunity for reaching young adults for Christ. But it also required much sacrifice from my wife to stay home a lot with carpet chewing kids.

One weekend in the summer I brought a large group of teens to have a camp out in my dad's backyard before we went to Cedar Point Amusement Park the next day. My parents lived really close to Cedar Point and so instead of making the youth trip one long grueling day trip to Ohio and back, we made a stop at my folk's house. We set up five large tents around a big campfire which were occupied by loud screaming teens. My dad made a bunch of hot dogs and opened up his pool so the students could have some fun things to do. After I helped him clean up, he called me inside the house and asked me one simple question, "Chris, your ministry with teens is great and all, but isn't it time for you to grow up?" That is all he said.

Boy, was I mad—hopping mad—but I didn't tell him. The next day as I was leading the pack of crazy teens through the amusement park, I keep thinking about what my dad said. And the more I thought about it, the more I knew he was right. It was time for me to move on, to use more of my gifts, to take on a bigger challenge. He wasn't saying that youth ministry was a bad thing, he was simply telling me I was called for something different. The more I thought about it the more I also realized my family needed more of me than they were getting. His simple question tore through me like a bullet to the heart, and it made me question my motives and decisions.

A few months later an opportunity came up for me to consider taking on the role of lead pastor, and because of my dad's prompting, my heart was already prepared to transition out and move on. And I was ready. Just further proof that a dad's words are truly powerful. And when used correctly, they can help turn a boy into a man and a girl into a woman that is prepared to take on the world.

Psalm 112:2 promises that a man who fears God will have children that are "mighty in the land." They will be strong because a dad was not afraid to use strong words with his children. Truth is hard to speak, but a good dad will always say what needs to be said.

CASTING A VISION

Grace and truth are such a potent mixture that when the combination is just right, a dad's words will be so compelling they can change a life. This is especially true when it comes to talking about the future with your son or daughter. Grace listens to the heart of a child, it gives the father the ability to hear what a child wants, and it sees what a child can do. Truth applies what it learns and speaks that vision back to the child. Often a father is so consumed with his own life that he doesn't have the patience to study how his children have been designed by God. But grace does.

Most fathers I know expect their children to fulfill the parent's dreams and wishes. If dad grew up loving basketball often the child is pushed in that same direction, where they are taken to hundreds of camps, forced to join school teams, and the parent will shell out hundreds of dollars to help them be successful as their dad counts success. I have seen some parents continue to push even if their child doesn't have the skill or desire to play. It becomes a sad tragedy when those children fail and resent their parents for pushing so hard. Instead of encouragement, they only feel judgment and disappointment. This is the surest way to crush a soul.

But a good dad sees his child as God's child first, designed by him for a purpose only he or she can fulfill. A good father then communicates that to their child and lets them know they have their blessing.

When it came to sports, my dad was exceptional. He didn't need to live his dreams through me, so he let me decide if I wanted to play them or not. When he went to my ball games, he was content to simply be a spectator and watch without making it about him. Thankfully, he let me be me.

I loved sports but when you don't have the body of a high-performance athlete, sports will come to an end. A good father will help a son through that reality. But when it came to business, my dad unknowingly pushed me into his field of expertise. That is all he knew so that is where he encouraged me to go. But after a few miserable years of struggle and failure in sales, I eventually worked up the courage to tell my dad that his calling wasn't mine.

It shocked him. He wasn't angry, just sad that I did not find the same joy he did in the business world. I was frightened to tell him the truth because I was not sure how he would respond, but when I finally explained it to him through a stream of hot tears, his love for me was more important than his dreams for me. He immediately saw my frustration and the pain I was feeling and encouraged me to pursue what I believed God was calling me to.

Slowly God revealed to me that ministry was the calling he placed on my life. My passion for the Bible and teaching others his truth lit me on fire, and my dad saw it. Even though he didn't understand it, nor was he called to it, he supported me in it. Grace allowed him to listen and encourage me and the truth helped him to clearly see how God made me different than him.

After I was firmly established in the church where I am now, the congregation asked me to be the lead pastor. My dad came to the installation and I asked him to speak. When he stood up to the pulpit on stage he expressed how excited he was for me and encouraged the congregation to love and support me. Even though ministry was not his field of expertise, he knew it was where God wanted me and he applauded my success in it.

That is all a child wants—to please their dad. And I can say, though we are different in calling, ability and skill, through his words of affirmation I know he was proud of me. That is all I ever really wanted.

ELEVEN:
The Opposite Sex

"Treat younger men as brothers, older women as mothers,
and younger women as sisters, with absolute purity."
— *Titus 5:2*

Growing up in the Weeks' house there were three unspoken things my brother and I knew my dad hated: Disrespecting your parents, using bathroom humor, and hitting your sisters. If he ever caught us laughing at brown-stained poop jokes or enjoying vile swear words he would immediately look our way and with his booming voice say, "I never want to hear you laugh at that kind of trash ever again in this house." Even when I had my friends over, he wouldn't let them off the hook when they were being crass when it came to bowel movements and bodily discharges. And you didn't ever talk back to him. If you wanted to see what the face of a charging bull looks like, all you had to do is show a small hint of disrespect toward my dad and that look of danger would appear on his face. All of us kids knew that look. And when we saw it, we ran across the railroad tracks behind our house or hid down in the darkest corner of the basement not wanting to be found.

But there was one rule, one line of demarcation, one fatherly decree you made sure you would never cross. My brother and I knew we were never, and I mean never, ever, allowed to hit our sisters. My dad made this unbreakable law crystal clear, "Guys don't hit girls!" Call it chivalry, old-fashioned ethics, male chauvinism, whatever you like, it didn't matter, we just knew violence against women was off-limits. And my sisters also knew it. And sometimes, in small ways, they would test these limits with their little brother 'Chrissy' (the name they gave me when they wanted to drive me crazy) and they knew I should not, nor would not, under any conditions, strike back.

Now let me be fair. Because they knew I wouldn't hit back they would not push this demand too far, but sometimes they did test how mad they could make me. They would sing a song that drove me crazy, "Christopher Joseph, four weeks old, how do you like the world so far?" After they would sing it, I would want to strangle them, but they knew I wouldn't. Not only was I too scared of my dad, but my three sisters were older than me and would gang up on me, so I had no chance fighting against them.

I can remember a time when my sisters were babysitting, and as the youngest kid I refused to clean the dishes after dinner. It was my chore for the night and they demanded that I do it. I was stubborn and said, "Make me!" So they chased me around the house and when they caught me, my sister Steph pinned me by the arms on a chair while Gina smeared wet cat food all over my face. I was furious! I chased them and wanted to hit them, but they looked at me and said, "Remember Chris, boys don't hit girls!" They won, and I had no other choice but to do the dishes.

From the moment of birth, my world was filled with sisters. I was surrounded and often outmatched by the female gender. My dad always insisted that I treat them as equals, and as the youngest, they were most of the time my superiors. I learned quickly that anything I could do my sisters could usually do better. And my dad always treated us the same in value and ability.

When he wanted to lose weight and start a jogging routine, he asked my sister Steph to help him. When he needed help with his taxes my sister Tam was always the one to come to the rescue. When he wanted someone to argue with about anything, Gina was there to debate. And when he needed someone to sit in the garage attic to sweat with him, that was my job. There was never a patriarchal divide in our home. If anything, my dad was an equally fair devil's advocate towards us all. He loved to challenge us to think and use our minds. He especially enjoyed making all of us angry. And when he wanted to just sit and have stimulating conversation, the whole family was to be included. I could never imagine life without the joy my sisters brought.

It is often said that most of life is caught and not taught, and from watching how my dad interacted with my mom and four sisters on a daily basis, I learned important truths about the female gender that are never really discussed in our politically correct society. In fact, I have always wondered why feminism and fighting for equal rights was such a big deal. Then I realized not every woman was treated in their homes the same way my sisters were by my dad. But if they were, this constant battle for "hegemony" or "control" over the other gender would never have spiraled into the lunacy that it has become today. Here are the three major truths I have learned about women because of my dad.

ONE: Women, as well as Men, are Image Bearers

Genesis 1:27 couldn't be clearer on this point, "So God created mankind in his own image, in the image of God he created them; male and female he created them." Image means that God has imprinted himself on the heart of every human. And because of this, each person is priceless. Genesis 9:6 also states, "Whoever sheds human blood, by humans shall their blood be shed; for in the image of God has God made mankind." Human beings carry the likeness of God, we are each the pinnacle of God's creative genius, and we alone can have communion in our spirit with him. This includes both men and women alike. There is no superiority of worth and value, both genders Jesus came to purchase with his blood. Revelation 5:9 screams this, "You are worthy to take the scroll and to open its seals, because you were slain, and with your blood you purchased for God persons (men and women) from every tribe and language and people and nations."

Even 1 Peter 3:7 is solid on this point, "Husbands, in the same way be considerate as you live with your wives, and treat them with respect as the weaker partner and heirs with you of the gracious gift of life, so that nothing will hinder your prayers." If you look closely, Peter does recognize differences in male and female design, but there is equality in their value. That is the key for men to understand. We must start every relationship by seeing God's placement of his price tag—both men and women are heirs of life. Christian men and women will both rule and reign with Jesus in heaven. For that reason, men need to be both considerate and respectful to women. And respect means we are to recognize that though there are areas we are made different, instead of making it an issue of who is better or worse, we need to rather help carry each other's load.

When someone is an image-bearer we have to be very careful not to degrade or destroy that particular aspect of beauty concerning God's image they have been given. Jesus says something in Matthew 5:22 that speaks to the importance of image-bearing, listen very closely, "I tell you that anyone who is angry with a brother or sister will be subject to judgment. Again, anyone who says to a brother or sister, 'Raca,' is answerable to the court. And anyone who says, 'You fool!' will be in danger of the fire of hell." Why will someone be in danger of the fires of hell for calling a person a fool, an idiot, a contemptible piece of trash? Because no one is trash, no one is to be treated as an expendable resource simply for the pleasure of others. No one is to be used. And if you notice, Jesus says this includes all women, who are your sisters!

My dad always respected my sisters as God's daughters. They had incredible value and worth. He insisted that they be treated with respect and dignity by their brothers and boyfriends too. He often would make sure the boys who came over to talk with my sisters were guys he could trust and who valued my sisters. If my sisters dressed inappropriately, he would tell them to respect themselves first if they wanted guys to respect them. They were not objects to be used or owned, they were human beings made in God's image.

Even the shows and movies he watched he made sure were respectful to women. He was impressed by the class of a Grace Kelly and the exquisite haunting beauty of a Sophia Loren, but when a woman was used and devalued themselves for the sheer pleasure of male beasts and ignorant brutes he was quickly incensed. Sure, he noticed a beautiful woman, but he never ogled or taught his sons to lust after their beauty. Pornography was strictly forbidden in our house, and likewise, he was not impressed by lecherous men who would boast about their female conquests. I remember when he had some married couples come over for dinner and one man, in particular, would always make inappropriate comments toward women. I thought my dad was going to rip his head off.

God gave to him the heart of a good father who loved his daughters immensely and wanted the best for them. And he showed that respect for them started with the clear example he gave in the home. He was not a fundamentalist prude that wanted women wearing burkas and dresses at all times, but he was a person of class. He wanted his daughters to enhance their dignity and worth with what they wore, and not lower it by dressing like a scantily clad hussy. And he definitely didn't want his sons chasing women who dressed in such demeaning fashion as well.

TWO: Women as Friends

Because women were image-bearers and not primarily to be seen as objects of desire he had no trouble treating his daughters as his best friends. I once read that fathers who have lust problems don't know how to be friends with their daughters. But my dad didn't have either of these problems. He could talk to women without them feeling ignored or treated simply as a piece of meat at the local buyer's market. They were unique individuals that had dreams, talents, important life experiences, and expertise. He was happy to admit that my mom was the smartest person in our house. He loved to boast that she was an editor of a local college paper and could read and understand books he couldn't even pronounce. He also let her handle the bills and important financial affairs of the house because he knew she was much more gifted in that area than he was at it.

I will never forget when my dad met a small fundamentalist pastor who clearly felt men were the superior sex. My dad would point out to me how the pastor would not even talk to women in the church or look them in the eye because he felt above them in station. He called the pastor an "Islamic-Baptist". I asked him what that meant. He said true Christianity treats women as equals. Jesus would even care about the soul of the prostitutes and peasant women where they could go to him and find grace and mercy. And after women found grace and mercy, he let them be a huge part of the early church: Mary Magdalen was the first to see him in the garden, Anna helped fund the disciples, and Lydia started the first church in Philippi. But when some Christian men and leaders cannot even look at women in the eye it tells you two things: Either they are very threatened by women who are more capable and talented than they are, or they have no self-control when it comes to the opposite sex. So instead of talking with women, because the small man is either embarrassed or attracted to them, the Islamic-Baptist male simply will ignore women altogether. My dad would say the more ignorant a man is the worse they treat women.

Growing up in my father's home, I naturally found that my sisters became my best friends. We loved spending time together, and being the youngest, I learned so much from them. Tammy, my oldest sister, taught me about good music like *Bread, Crosby, Stills, Nash and Young*, and of course *Jim Croce*. Gina would introduce me to Saturday afternoon scary movies and buying good candy, she especially loved *Bit-O-Honey* and *Twizzlers*. And Stephanie was my co-explorer of the Lake Erie shoreline and the beautiful trails of Cleveland Metro Parks. Stephanie was also my fellow classmate. If there was a girl that was interested in me at school, Stephanie was the one who always had my back and gave me the low-down if the girl was right for me or not. I have a sneaking suspicion when a girl liked me that my sister Stephanie didn't like, she and my other sister Gina would threaten and warn them not to talk to their baby brother or they would have some serious words. I always wondered why it was hard to have a girlfriend in High School, but now I think I know why.

Stephanie also loved to play pranks on the boys in our school and she let me join in on it with her. One of my favorite memories was when a boy named Kevin kept coming over to our house because he liked her. One day my sister had enough of Kevin and told me to get rid of him, but he wouldn't leave until he talked to Stephanie himself. So Stephanie told me to ask him if he wanted some candy. And while I was talking to him, she went inside and took some lemon drops, rolled them in fiery-hot tabasco sauce, and sprinkled them with a heavy dose of garlic powder. After rewrapping them she came outside and gave Kevin the candy. When he started sucking on it you could see his mouth was burning up, and it was then he realized that Steph did not like him, so he spit out the demon candy and sped off on his ten-speed bike. He never came over again. There was and still is no one like my sister Stephanie.

THREE: Partners in Promise

The final thing I learned about women is that God designed the right one for the man as a partner for life. My mom and dad were not just friends, but they were teammates. As I already shared, they clearly were attracted to each other. And after saying I do; they became true partners in life. Their relationship was never one of competition but it was built on cooperation. The Battle of the Sexes was only a stupid idea you watched on television and read about in gossip columns. And extreme feminism was nothing but the Devil's idea to divide and conquer. But real life, living in the muck and mire of everyday marriage, took total and absolute teamwork. To survive, you needed a partner you could completely trust and count on. That is how God designed it. It is not a competition, it is not an exploitation, but rather it is a covenant of love. And the covenant is to be formed with the person you know you can enter the fiercest battle and storm with and overcome.

My sister Laura Lee is a case in point. To raise a severely mentally handicapped daughter my parents needed to lean and rely on each other. And not only that, but raising five children alongside Laura, was a task that required every ounce of their blood, sweat, and tears in order for their marriage and family to thrive. I remember my mom doing some research on my sister Laura's disease and she found out that couples who had a daughter with Rett Syndrome had more than a 70% chance of getting a divorce. Trying to simply live with a handicapped child was no easy task, and to reduce their marriage down to a battle between genders is like claiming that fighting World War 2 was a matter of saying which army was better, the British or the Americans. Both were needed to defeat Hitler.

My parent's favorite song that they played often, because they said it exemplified their relationship, was "Through the Years," by Kenny Rogers. Here are some of the lyrics,

I can't remember when you weren't there
When I didn't care for anyone but you
I swear we've been through everything there is
Can't imagine anything we've missed
Can't imagine anything the two of us can't do

Through the years
You've never let me down
You turned my life around
The sweetest days I've found
I've found with you
Through the years
I've never been afraid
I've loved the life we've made
And I'm so glad I've stayed
Right here with you
Through the years.

Why do people fall for such silly and stupid narratives like feminism, or homophobia, or even transgenderism when marriage is a covenant relationship between two people that have eternal consequences? God designed men and women to continue the task of raising image-bearers who are going to live with him in the heavenly kingdom. And since this is true, the male and female relationship takes serious consideration and thought. Much more thought than being attracted to someone over an Instagram photo, or a drunken one-night-stand. You are looking for a partner for life.

I remember walking in the woods with my dad one sunny Saturday afternoon. He said, "Chris, there are some things that you need to look for in a woman if you are going to find the life partner that will stick with you until the end."

I was curious, so I asked, "Wow, what are they?"

"These are not politically correct, but they are five qualities you want in a partner if you are going to form a home with them." He picked up a stick and threw it to our dog Grizzly Bear who was walking with us.

"Number one, you want to have a similar worldview. That includes a culture you both understand. I am not talking about the same race or ethnicity; I'm talking about values. You need to see life the same way, have the same dreams, want the same things." Grizzly dropped the stick, and he threw it again.

He continued, "This leads directly to number two and three. You need to find a person that believes in the same God you do. It is the Holy Spirit that really brings you together during the difficult times. If your spouse doesn't worship Jesus, then you will not be united in the biggest parts of life. You will have no vocabulary to express the joys and struggles. So number three, look at the way her family celebrates and practices their religion. There needs to be some familiarity with the way you practically live your life with God. I am not talking about denominations, but actual living. If someone dies and their family has no real hope in the afterlife then you are left in a vacuum. Watch her parents, and especially her mom, because more times than not she will adopt the same values that her mom has."

"That makes sense," I replied. "What are the last two?"

"Well, number four is to look for someone that has similar interests. That is pretty simple. Life is meant to be fun, and if you can't have fun together it makes for a long marriage. But the last one is this, marry someone that has the same intelligence quotient as you. You don't want to marry someone who thinks themselves smarter than you because they will always carry a sense of superiority that will suck the life out of a soul. While at the same time you also don't want someone content with being simple-minded. You need to be pushed and challenged, life is meant to be explored and understood. A simple-minded person will only be about trivial matters, like acquiring possessions and looking good to the neighbors. That gets exhausting. You want someone that thinks, uses their brain, and confronts you when you need it. You want someone who makes you better!" He then threw the stick to

Grizz one more time, then added, "In other words, you want a best friend."

I thought long and hard about that last statement over the years. And now every time I read Genesis 2:18 I see it in a new light, "The Lord God said, 'It is not good for the man to be alone. I will make him a helper suitable for him.'" That is it! The opposite sex isn't given for silly sexual games, they are not given to compete to show which gender wins, who is better, and who is stronger. They are given for something so much more important, to display the Glory of God, to show his image to others so the world will watch and wonder. Wow, what a task, what a noble enterprise. And most of all, what a wonderful design!

TWELVE:
Love Listens

"To answer before listening—
that is folly and shame."
— Proverbs 18:13

This is the chapter I have been most excited to write because it concerns the one thing that my dad has given to me as an inheritance. It does not concern money, it does not contain details about a precious heirloom passed down from his father's father, nor is it about a cabin in the Caymans. But the gift that he gave me is what really defined him both as a wonderful father and a man. I believe it is also something that set him apart from other men. And over the course of time, he has passed this heirloom on to all of his children. It is the art of listening. He was a master at this and he modeled and taught it to all of his children. Because he knew how to listen, all sorts of people opened up their hearts to him. Often the strangest people were his friends all because my dad took the time to lend them his ear.

I once had a conversation with my dad about making friends. He said to me, "Chris, do you want to be known as a great conversationalist? Do you want to be liked and invited places? Learn how to listen. I have found you can spend a whole evening with a person and you don't even need to say a thing. But afterward they will say that you were the most interesting person they have ever met."

With a curious look, I asked my dad, "How is that possible? If you don't speak, how can you be interesting?"

"Simple," my dad replied, "Because people love talking about themselves, and when you are genuinely interested in them as a person, they will find you fascinating. I know, it sounds backward, but it is true."

"But dad, isn't that manipulating people? Just listening to them in order to be liked by them?"

"Oh no," he said, "You don't listen to manipulate, you listen to show love. Every person is special, uniquely designed by God. Listening is the tool God has given us to learn about and explore the vast variety of people. Sadly, no one takes the time or effort to listen anymore, which is why we live in such a lonely world."

A LONELY WORLD

I had a friend named Buddy. He was a wonderful guy with an extremely sad soul. One night my wife and I invited him over for dinner, we served him some sandwiches and hot soup. We all shared a lot of laughs and fun stories, the conversation flowed freely and the laughter was spontaneous and good. Later in the evening Buddy looked out the window from our living room and said, "I am not sure if people really know me. In fact, in my whole life, I am not sure if I have ever been known."

My wife then asked, "Buddy, what do you mean?"

And with a heavy sigh he said, "No one has actually tried to get to know me. To listen to me. To understand me." And then he said, "I am not sure anybody is ever really known on this earth."

It was a sad statement, but a painfully honest one. I have never forgotten it. And I believe if most people would feel honest enough to share what is on their hearts, they would express similar sentiments. We live in a terribly lonely world; people daily pass each other without ever being known or feeling known. Scripture says this is true because sin has caused a general slide in human society toward alienation. Sin doesn't just separate us from God himself, but it has built up a massive wall that isolates human beings from each other. Titus 3:3 perfectly describes alienation by saying that before Christ comes into someone's life, "We lived in malice and envy, being hated and hating one another." Sting writes in the song *Message in the Bottle*:

> *Just a castaway, an island lost at sea, oh*
> *Another lonely day, with no one here but me, oh*
> *More loneliness than any man could bear*
> *Rescue me before I fall into despair, oh*
> *I'll send an S.O.S to the world*
> *I'll send an S.O.S to the world*
> *I hope that someone gets my*

I hope that someone gets my
I hope that someone gets my
Message in a bottle, yeah

We are all castaways lost at sea and as a result, we all want to be known and understood. We long to have just one or two people who care enough to listen to our message that is bound up in this bottle called a human being. But we are all so busy, which makes for a lonely world.

Last year, Buddy was undergoing total physician care as a result of having a severe case of brain cancer, while at the same time, he was also enduring traumatic emotional suffering from the pain of a recent divorce. After just a few months of living in a total care facility, he fell, breaking his pelvis, which ended up putting him on life support where he was fighting for his life. To make matters even more critical, he was diagnosed with Covid-19. In some of his correspondence with me during this time he wrote, "I have extreme moments of WHY toward God. But then I feel awful. I just want to parent my kids. Now I am so limited with my infirmities. Even before having Covid, I could only see them twice a week. Ultimately, I do trust his Sovereignty. I just don't understand…"

But in spite of his pain, he took the effort to encourage me concerning the more minor struggles going on in my life. The last thing he wrote me before he died was this; "I'm glad the Lord is using me to encourage you. My life has changed so drastically overnight that I oftentimes don't know if I'm doing anything that is glorifying to Him." A week after that short text he died in a sterile hospital bed without his kids, a broken marriage, single, and completely alone. All he really wanted was to be known by others and be used by God, but he was not even sure if his life mattered.

There are people like Buddy all around us. And what is worse, there are children in your home that feel the same way. Sad and lonely people looking for one person to listen. Will you, as a father, listen? Listening is rare. I think people like Buddy feel so isolated because people only know how to talk about themselves. And when they are not talking about themselves, they are being entertained by their phone, a television show, or they have headphones covering their ears, listening to the newest song or podcast. As a result, people like Buddy are lost and forgotten.

Listening is the easiest and most effective tool God has given each of us to reach the broken and the lost. I once heard it said that the reason God gave us two ears, two eyes, and one mouth was so that we can spend most of our time watching and listening, rather than speaking. Listening opens doors and exposes the secrets that people have kept locked up and hidden, just waiting for that one person they can trust to share their priceless treasures with.

Philippians 2:3 says that we are to treat others better than ourselves, and listening does this. In truth, listening takes humility, especially when it comes to listening to your children. In order to listen, you must first admit you do not know as much about a person as you probably think you do. We are masters at pre-judging people and making blind assessments of their situations. Pop-psychology and woke culture has conditioned us to be that way. We think we know someone because we can put them in a predetermined box —the color of their skin, their gender, their race, their religion, their birth order, their enneagram score—but this is both dangerous and arrogant. Instead of being allowed into the mysterious caverns of the human soul, we get locked out by our own pride.

And this is where my dad's gift comes in: listening is love.

THE HUMAN CAVE

People are fascinating! Have you ever "people-watched" in a mall or sat and noticed the amazing array of different body types and personalities at a carnival or amusement park? Have you ever taken the time to realize that the people living in your house with you are filled with amazing ideas and opinions? In fact, the more I know my children, the more I begin to learn just how different and mysterious they are. This is because each person carries a totally unique facet of God's image that only they were created with. This is where my dad taught me about the particular, not just general, worth of the human soul.

Each individual displays a different side of God's creative genius that no one else can. Scientists like to dumb everything down by telling us that a human being is predetermined by only two variables: (1) Nature; which includes the genetic makeup of the person, and (2) Nurture; the environmental situations and circumstances that a person is born into. But according to scripture, we are so much more than merely biological machines acting on chemical influences and conditioned like we are some kind of behavioristic robot. God's word says we are not simply making daily decisions out of some vague evolutionary impulse we learned over eons and eons of time; we are something so much more—we are image-bearers. There is mystery and depth to each of us that one simple psychological test or human genome study cannot adequately capture.

No two people are ever the same. In each human heart there is a myriad of unique twists and turns that no other person possesses, and to try to force a complex human being into a predetermined box is to do violence to their dignity. 1 Peter 1:22 tells us to "love each other deeply from the heart." And to go deep you need the time and tools to properly understand the richness of the human heart. To do that we need to learn how to go spiritual spelunking; we need to become cave explorers of the soul through the art of listening.

Imagine you are in a room where a group of people are talking. Now look in the corner. Do you see that person who is sitting alone with arms crossed tight and downcast in spirit? Can you feel the invisible icy wall of protection that has formed all around them? Everyone feels it. And as a result, no one will approach them, it takes too much effort. So instead, we gravitate toward the familiar and friendly faces, those that are easy to hang out with, those that offer some positive response in return. The lover of Christ, however, is drawn to the downtrodden and lowly. So instead of responding like everyone else and avoiding them, you decide to take this person on as a challenge, "I am going to get them to talk to me." The hardest nut to crack usually hides the biggest reward. But how do you get invited in?

My dad would often say "people don't care how much you know; they simply want to know how much you care." And that is where it starts. If you only talk about yourself, you will be met with resistance and more stonewalling from the sad and lonely person sitting in the corner. Only the person who wants to unlock the door of the heart can break the barrier. And it begins with questions laced with sincerity:

- Who is this person?
- What do they like? What do they dislike?
- How do they feel? What excites them? Why are they so sad?
- What are their hopes and dreams?

If you don't know the person, start with a simple introduction—make the first move. Then ask a question as if it were a special key that has been given to you to unlock the heart...and then wait. If the lock doesn't open, try another key. Some locks snap right open while others have five or six latches, including heavy bolts and iron bars. But keep asking. Often all it takes is the single right question, so don't give up!

STEP ONE: Enjoy the Person's Answers in Order to Stay as a Welcomed Visitor

This is the tough part. When you get an answer or small tidbit about the person's life, enjoy it. Relish it. Most people at this point do one of two things: (1) they don't really hear or they respond with, "Oh that's nice." And then move on. (2) They use a person's answer as a springboard to tell their own story. Don't, I repeat, *don't* talk about yourself at this stage. There is nothing worse than sharing your heart and then having the person listening only using it as fodder to talk about themselves. A person who offers a precious tidbit and then is ignored will only shut down and the rest of your keys will prove useless.

But if you treasure their information and take it in, you will continue to be lead down the dark corridors of their cave where there are more doors to be opened. When you hear and enjoy what a person tells you, the person will open up like never before. My dad would just listen for a while as he asked me questions, taking in every word. If I told him about my friends, he remembered their names. If I described an event, he remembered the high and low points. If I shared a frustration, he saw my anguish. Which leads to…

STEP TWO: Empathize with Hurts, Injustice, and Mistreatment

Always remember that, initially, a person's perspective is truth to them. When people share things that may be awkward or even controversial, don't immediately judge or mock them or write them off, even if you completely disagree with what they say. Your objective is building trust—not winning an argument. Listening and understanding doesn't mean agreeing, it means you care about the person. That was the hallmark of Christ. The woman he met at the well in John 4 was living in obvious sin. Instead of condemnation, Christ met her with compassion. And as a result, she was receptive to his message of grace that he offered a few minutes later. Her life was changed forever from one simple encounter with Jesus. If you are a Christian, this same Jesus lives in you too.

My dad was a master at this. He had six children who were all different and the friends we brought home all were able to connect with my dad in the oddest of ways. My oldest sister Tammy had pot-smoking hippies for friends with long hair and bell-bottom jeans. They talked to my dad and told them all about their life. My sister Gina had an array of cool and popular friends that came over and my dad enjoyed them even in their silly pretensions. My nerdy humble friends always brightened up with my dad because they knew he knew them.

This skill has been the bread and butter of my ministry as a pastor. One time I had a couple come into my office for counseling. I first wanted to get to know them and here is how they first described themselves, "We are Big Foot hunters, and we are convinced that one day he will be found and proven as true." I wanted to laugh, but they really believed it. If I treated them as if I thought they were crazy they would never open up or talk to me again, but over the years they became really good friends of mine.

STEP THREE: Invited into the Soul's Cellar

When people first open up, they will tell you things that are relatively safe and neutral. Initial information in a conversation will always be a tad bit trivial because it is the only way a person can test the waters of trust. If you don't care about a person's small stuff, you have no right to enter into the dark secrets hidden deep in the cellar of the soul. If someone starts out talking about sports and you think sports are stupid and a waste of time, they will shut down. But if you really listen to the reason they like sports, soon you may hear them tell you stories about how their dad took them to a football game when they were seven and it reminds them of great days, or how they gained confidence about themselves. Now those sorts of things are not trivial. So if the initial information is treated as precious to you, the person will begin to feel safe and may invite you in to hear deeper and darker things. It is in the cellar where the monsters dwell. And when you are invited down there, this is when a person begins to feel known.

I was always amazed when my friends would tell my dad about their home life after just coming over a few times. They felt safe to ask him questions and get advice on how to handle the confusion they faced in life. He would ask them to sit down at the kitchen table and share some peanuts and they would talk. Some of the loneliest people would end up laughing and talking like they knew my dad forever. When my sister's hippie girlfriend was rushed to the hospital for drinking a bottle of turpentine after smoking some bad weed, it was my dad she called to have him drive her to the hospital to help her.

Listening allows you in and down. And when you make it into the cellar of a soul, this is where God enters. We have the mistaken belief that we need to win arguments if people are ever going to accept God. We think apologetics is the route to conversion, but God has come to save, not win logical debates. Sin festers like black mold in the basement of a soul, and when you are allowed down to expose the light of Christ, people are changed. The truth is, Jesus is the only answer to a dark lonely heart. As he once said, "it is not the healthy who need a doctor, but the sick."

EXPERTS IN THEIR OWN WORLD

More than anything, listening says "You matter to me, you are important." Scripture is very clear about how words from a fool gush out like dirty sewer water and don't take the time to stop and listen. "Fools have no interest in understanding, they only want to air their own opinions." (Proverbs 18:2) But love wants to know the other. And your children want to be known the most.

One of the greatest benefits from listening that I saw in my dad was that it allowed a person to be the expert in their own world. If you let yourself learn from someone it validates their significance. Too often parents, and people in general, have to be the experts. They often demand to be heard and strong-arm people to listen to them—respect isn't earned, it is enforced. Instead of opening their children up, it causes them to hide in their cave more, and double bolt each lock they already had on the doors of their soul. And the parent will never be allowed down into the cellar, that is for sure.

But when a parent listens and wants to learn, the child loves it. My dad was a great college football player, so he had both years of experience and learning from some top-notch coaches. When I started playing football in the 7th grade I would come home and my dad would ask me about practice. He wanted to know my position, the offense we ran, and the things I was learning. I can remember saying, "Dad, I don't need to tell you what it's like, you played a whole lot longer than I did." He said, "But Chris, I never played on your team, I never had your coaches, and I'm interested in learning." Most fathers yell and tell their kids how to be better, my dad wanted to learn. And then when I asked him how I could improve, he answered me from the situation at hand instead of some nostalgic memory of the past. Wisdom applies solutions in the present, arrogance and pride force solutions from the past.

No one wants to hear, "Been there, done that." But rather we long to hear, "Tell me how you are doing, because I have never really experienced what you are going through." Listening takes patience and love, and good listeners expand the souls of their children. It is a lonely world out there; do you have time enough to listen?

THIRTEEN:
Enter the Dragon

*"For I dreaded destruction from God,
and for fear of his splendor I could not do such things."*
— Job: 31:23

This is the chapter I have had the hardest time putting to paper because it concerns an issue that you are not allowed to even mention in our current popular culture where "coddling" has been defined as "compassion" and "pampering" has replaced "true parenting." This topic has been labeled as toxic and potentially abusive by both progressive sociologists and feminists alike in hopes of muzzling strong men forever. And it is this topic that I believe we desperately need to restore in order to have a healthy home life, and a true father designed by God leading the families once again.

If you watch current TV and movies, a dad no longer matters. He has become a plaything instead of a parent, a money maker and not a man. But according to scripture, a dad is meant to lead, but he is also sometimes meant to frighten. He is the one person who is to draw the lines in the sand that his children know they are not allowed to cross, to restrain the storm that sometimes rages in the heart of a rebellious child.

A dad is a steward. He is to model an aspect of God that we rarely talk about—his holiness. Habakkuk 1:13 says that God's eyes are so pure he cannot look upon evil. This means God is a being that is not to be trifled with, and he definitely will not trifle with sin. We need to tread lightly when we enter his presence because he is the God who causes the mountains to smoke and the nations to tremble. Theologians use a phrase to describe the holiness of God, "mysterium tremendum." This is what a creature experiences when they approach the untamed nature of God. "Mysterium tremendum" is having a feeling of terror, but also being spellbound with utter fascination. You want to draw close to God out of wonder, but at the same time, you know you better be careful the closer you get. In a small way, a good father offers a teeny tiny dose of this from time to time with his children. I believe a healthy fatherly fear is both comforting and the key to forming strong character in his children.

BROKEN HOMES

In the summer of 2020, crowds of rampaging anarchists set fire to the streets of America to protest against police brutality and what they viewed as societal injustice. Instead of following the peaceful examples of the civil rights protestors in the past, these new groups took a more aggressive approach in demanding change by using looting and violence to get their point across. Report after report showed students as young as 14 and 15 to no older than 26 were the ones being arrested for causing billions of dollars worth of damage to local businesses, government buildings, and general harassment of common everyday citizens. Some of these protestors would stop traffic on major highways and thoroughfares causing massive disruptions in business and commerce. These groups even ignored the social distancing requirements that were required by the CDC and HHS to try and stop the spread of the deadly Covid-19.

Many pundits wondered why the new protests in our society resorted to such raw violence. Some pointed to the destructive nature of progressive politics, others to the anger born from economic inequities, and many defaulted to the years of racial tension. But if you were to look closely at the majority of those who were arrested, the most prevalent characteristics were that they were young, angry, and often came from broken homes. In truth, many of the protestors were previously involved in acts of violence.

Working with hundreds of students and families for the last 25 years as a pastor of a large church, it is no secret that children from broken, single-parent, and fatherless homes all have significant disadvantages compared to those being raised in a loving two-parent home. And one of the biggest problems with the children being raised in broken homes is not being able to curb their aggression and violence. As one *study says:

"Using data from the National Longitudinal Study of Adolescent Health explored the relationship between family structure and risk of violent acts in neighborhoods. The results revealed that if the number of fathers is low in a neighborhood, then there is an increase in acts of teen violence. The statistical data showed that a 1% increase in the proportion of single-parent families in a neighborhood is associated with a 3% increase in an adolescent's level of violence. In other words, adolescents who live in neighborhoods with lower proportions of single-parent families and who report higher levels of family integration commit less violence."

Why is this? The answer is very simple—dads who are present make a difference! Fathers have been given a God-given ability to tame the heart of their children in ways a mother never can. Forget all the politically correct sophistry, mothers and fathers are made differently. And I believe there is placed in the heart of a child an overwhelming, almost unquantifiable, desire to please their dad. Along with that desire is a natural fear that God placed there by design which is both physical and emotional. This is not an abusive, out-of-control kind of fear, but a fear born out of love and respect.

When a child has a good dad, they won't want to disappoint him while at the same time they will want to draw near to him. This fatherly fear, when used under the guidance of the Holy Spirit, is potent and wonderful. When it is under the influence of the flesh, this same fear can be abusive and may cause long-lasting emotional damage. Like the flame of a fireplace, when it is placed inside the cover and safety of a brick hearth, it provides heat, warmth, comfort, and fascination for the family. But if you were to throw the burning logs out of the fireplace and onto the living room floor, they will burn everything up—the carpet, drapes, couch, and even singe your shaggy dog sleeping in the corner. And no one likes the smell of burnt dog hair.

With great risk comes great reward. So it is with fatherly fear.

FATHERLY FEAR WARNS

Did you know that when God gives you children, they don't come fully trained? They are not preprogrammed computers with basic problem-solving algorithms hardwired in their heads. But rather, human brains for the first 12 years of life are gullible little blank gobs of goo. Teaching and training the child is the parent's job. You actually have to show them how to peel a banana, go to the bathroom, put on their shoes, and stay away from fire. Sometimes when a child is near a campfire, they can become mesmerized by the dancing colors of the flame. And like a charmed snake, they will slowly walk in a trance-like state with their small pudgy hands reaching for the enticing flames. Most moms will run to grab the child, but it is dad who can say with one loud word, "Jonny, Stop!" And instantly the child will snap out of the trance and stand there, stock-still.

There are more times than I can remember when a few strong words from my dad at just the right moment caused me to change my course of action. "Chris, you do not talk to your mother like that," "Chris, stop choking the dog with the leash," "Chris, quit riding your bike in the road", to "Chris, I never want to hear you say that word ever again!" When my mom told me "no" sometimes I heard it as a suggestion. When my dad said "no" it was a non-negotiable, carved in stone, line of demarcation.

I remember when my dad was teaching my sister Stephanie how to drive. She had a few months of driver's training before she could officially get her license. My dad let her drive around with her temporary license while he was in the passenger seat and I got to sit in the back. While driving down a side street by our house, my sister Steph took her eyes off the road and failed to make a proper stop at a stop sign. My dad instantly got hot. "Stephanie, pull over and stop the car!"

"Why, dad?" Steph innocently said. "It was a simple mistake."

"Just pull over." And when she pulled over, I was already cowering in the backseat because I knew a fast storm was breaking over my dad. "Stephanie, a car is not a toy. When you drive you must remember that every person in the car is placing their life in your hands. If you want to drive, you must drive defensively, you can't expect other people to stop for you. That is your responsibility. You can't play around. Do you understand?"

My sister gripped the wheel tighter holding back tears, "Yes, I understand."

After we started back up and Steph drove a little longer, my dad broke the silence and said, "Stephanie, I'm sorry I got so mad, but I'm your dad and you are my responsibility. I want to keep you alive. You know I love you, don't you?"

My sister nodded not saying a word, and she proceeded to drive slower than a grandma the rest of the way home. We all went into the house quiet as mice, the tension was still stiff in the air. Steph went upstairs, put on some sweats, and went running. I slinked into the living room to watch TV. In a few hours, the storm eventually passed, but the lesson stuck. When it was my time to drive a few years later, I never forgot that moment in the car, and I still remember it 40 years later, "Drive defensively, the car is not a toy!" A dad says the hard things, but always for our good.

FATHERLY FEAR QUESTIONS

If you were to ask people who is one of the most beloved characters in the Bible, King David is usually placed on the list of the top ten. He was a military hero, a King, a singer, a writer, and a man after God's own heart. But he also was terribly flawed. Everyone knows about his adulterous sin with Bathsheba or even when he numbered his troops out of pride. But very few people remember the biting accusation leveled against him found in the book of 1 Kings 1:6 when he never disciplined or rebuked his son by asking, "Why do you behave as you do?" Instead of steering and guiding his son Adonijah, he let him live a profligate life.

A good dad questions and butts into his children's lives. A good dad stands in the way of the arrogance of his children and makes them give an account for why they do the things they do. A good dad confronts the ever-present sin that is lurking behind the door of his child's heart. At the time no one likes their father's interference, but in the long run, you will look back and love him for it. This is what children miss from not having a dad.

Sometimes fathering takes just being aware and present. I can remember when I was around 17 and many of my friends were persuading me to experiment with underage drinking. I would go to beer parties and when I got home I knew my dad would be waiting up for me, sitting in the living room reading, ready to pepper me with all kinds of questions. One Sunday afternoon my dad was watching a football game in the living room and I went to the refrigerator to get a drink and there was half a bottle of white wine on the top shelf. So I tried to be sneaky and I mixed a little wine with some orange juice to see what it tasted like. I heard from my cool friends that this is how you make a screwdriver, and I wanted to be cool too. After I mixed the drink and closed the refrigerator door my dad immediately called out from the living room, "Chris, what are you drinking in there? Orange juice? Man, that sound good. I am really thirsty; can I have a quick sip just to cool my tongue a little?"

I said, "No, the orange juice tastes a bit spoiled, I will pour it out."

My dad smirked and said, "I never knew orange juice could spoil so fast. Your mom just bought that yesterday. Oh well." He caught me, but he was subtle about it. And I knew I should never try that again—he was too aware and I was too foolish.

I also remember when I first came to faith in Christ. My dad didn't let me off the hook with easy answers and trite phrases. I just learned the doctrine of "justification by faith alone" and I was telling him about how once a person is saved he has a promise from God that he will live with him forever. He decided to play Devil's advocate to see how much I really understood it. "So," he said, "it sounds like you can have your cake and eat it too."

"Dad, what do you mean?" I asked puzzled.

"Well, it sounds like all you have to do is believe in Jesus and you can go on your merry way. Do whatever you like. Since heaven is guaranteed, you don't need to obey anymore. At least when we were Catholics they taught us we were never sure of our salvation. Sounds to me like you are buying into easy believism." My dad knew he struck a nerve, but he kept at it. "How does the idea of once saved always saved make me a better person?" He let it land and left. Boy did my dad know how to make me mad, but I wanted to have a solid answer so I could prove his argument wrong. As a result, I began a quest to understand my faith like never before and I haven't stopped since.

His questions concerning both my behavior and my beliefs were intended to challenge my apathy. You needed to know why you believed things and then act accordingly. My dad did not like sloppy thinking nor lethargic living. If we had visitors, it was our duty to be hospitable. If we voted for a candidate, he wanted to know what our reasons were. If we didn't like someone we just met, he would challenge our judgmental and hard hearts. The best way I could describe this aspect of my dad is that he didn't make our life decisions easy, if he thought we were wrong he would let us know.

FATHERLY FEAR MAKES YOU STRONG

In the book "12 Rules for Life", author and renowned clinical psychologist, Jordan Peterson, speaks of the importance of standing strong in what you believe, "If you say no to your boss, or your spouse, or your mother, when it needs to be said, then you transform yourself into someone who can say no when it needs to be said. If you say yes when no needs to be said, however, you transform yourself into someone who can only say yes, even when it is very clearly time to say no. If you ever wonder how perfectly ordinary, decent people could find themselves doing the terrible things the gulag camp guards did, you now have your answer. By the time no seriously needed to be said, there was no one left capable of saying it." A good father helps you form strong beliefs.

One day we were sitting at the kitchen table. I was going to Bible School and my dad asked me a very emotional question. I could tell it weighed heavy on him and he wanted a straight answer. "Chris, I have a question for you." I thought to myself, *Oh no, here it comes.* "If you get married and have kids, will you send your children to Catholic school like I did with you?" I knew my answer was not going to please him and the sparks were going to fly. My mom was washing a few dishes in the sink nearby and I could tell she was extremely interested in the conversation because she turned the nozzle of the water down a tad so she could hear us better.

"Well Dad, when I have kids I will probably send them either to public school or a private Christian school." I swallowed and continued, "But I definitely will not send them to a Catholic school." I knew this is not the answer he wanted to hear. You could see the arch of his bushy eyebrows going up which meant he was getting ready for battle. He could be quite an intimidating man when he was battling ideas.

"What is wrong with sending your kids to a Catholic school that you would consider public school a better option?" He asked. "Does that mean all those years I sent you to Catholic grade school and the Catholic University was a waste of time? Are saying I raised you wrong?" The volume of his voice was definitely ratcheting up a few notches.

"Dad, I never said that! Actually, I am grateful for the way I was raised. Your question was specifically about how I was going to raise my kids and I am not Catholic anymore, so I won't raise them Catholic."

"What is wrong with Catholic school? What is wrong with the way you were raised?" I think I saw some smoke rising from his large nostrils. "Sounds to me like I failed you as a father."

I was getting mad now because he was twisting my words, "Dad, that's unfair. I never said you were a bad father, I never said you did wrong, but I'm saying that the God the Catholic church teaches is not the God I believe in. I would rather have my kids not taught anything compared to a false god. You don't want me to go against my convictions, do you?"

He knew I wouldn't budge. He didn't say anything after that, but got up and left the room. I looked at my mom and asked her, "Was I wrong? Did I disrespect him?" My mom smiled and said, "Chris, you were exactly right! It's just your dad's way to process his past. I think he needed to hear that because he understands that you know what you believe." She dried a plate and turned off the water, then she added, "Chris, he will come back and apologize, just watch."

About two hours later I was in the living room watching sports. My dad came in and sat next to me. He looked at me with kind and humble eyes and said, "Chris, you are right. Thanks for putting me in my place. I want you to know I am really proud of how you stand on your convictions and I wouldn't want you to go against what you believe. I love you Chris, and I am sorry I blew up at you." He then smiled, "If I could do it all over again, I wouldn't send you to Catholic school either."

"Dad, no problem. I love you too." As we continued watching the game something changed in me. It was one of the first times I really stood my ground against my dad and I didn't back down. Because of that battle of wits with my dad, it crystalized in my heart that my faith was my own and my convictions were my own. It took a good strong fight with the fiery dragon to become battle-tested. Over the years as a pastor and public figure I had to debate my position many times with people who disagreed with my positions, angry church members who didn't understand why I made the decisions I did, and skeptics online who simply like to be belligerent for belligerence's sake. Because I overcame the fear of standing toe to toe with my dad, the man who I loved more than anything and never wanted to disappoint, I soon learned I could stand the test with anyone.

Because he challenged me, I grew strong.

A STRONG DAD

A strong dad raises strong children who can stand their ground without taking offense. A weak dad raises arrogant children who are not used to conflict and either wither when people disagree or demand that the world see everything from their point of view. We live in a world where microaggressions and improper pronouns set people's teeth on edge. The public debating of ideas has become a hate crime, and any disparaging remark that shows up in the past can get a person fired in the present. We have coddled people to the point where many of the kids graduating high school these days are nothing more than thin-skinned mental midgets. Childhood and adolescence have been moved up five to ten more years. 18-year-olds used to be able to stand their ground, now it takes a person to reach the age of 30 before they can get into a conflict without collapsing into a fetal position on the floor.

We are now told we must tolerate any anti-social action no matter how silly or perverse it may seem. If a person wants to dress like a princess at work the boss must let her, or him for that matter. If an employer reprimands an employee in public, they now sue for emotional damages. If a person is late for work, it's usually someone else's fault. And most of the reason for this fallout in society is that dads are afraid to be fathers.

Yes, there is a danger of having a dragon for a dad, but if he is for you and has been tamed by the Spirit of God, one thing is for sure, you will never have much to fear. Not only will your enemies stay away, but he will always be able to start a nice fire in the fireplace and toast your marshmallows to a golden brown.

---

* *Knoester, C., & Hayne, D.A. (2005). "Community context, social integration into family, and youth violence." Journal of Marriage and Family 67, 767-780.*

FOURTEEN:
The Greatest Gift of All

*"An overseer, then, must be above reproach,
the husband of one wife, temperate, prudent,
respectable, hospitable, and able to teach."*
— *1 Timothy 3:2*

One of the worries I have had in writing this book is that I may be accused of hero-worship; of painting an unrealistic picture of my dad as a man without stain, wrinkle, or blemish. But he would be the first one to deny that he was worthy of receiving any kind of adulation and praise. In fact, he often considered himself one of the most flawed men who ever lived. He would only really talk about himself if it included some kind of self-deprecating humor or embarrassing story. Some of my favorite stories he told were the ones that made him look bad.

One story in particular that always made him laugh out loud with the rest of us was when he went jogging with my sister Steph on a spring Saturday morning and he had a bad case of the "Turkey Trots" *(aka diarrhea).* They both set out on a ten-mile jog wearing thin jogging shorts and tank-tops. After just a few minutes of being gone from the house, I saw my dad sprinting back up the street at full speed. I was cutting the grass at the time and when he reached our house he sprinted across the front lawn and jumped behind a row of bushes. My sister was running superfast behind him and I asked her what was going on. "He has the Turkey Trots!" She said.

"Steph!" My dad shouted out, "Turn on the hose and bring it over here!"

So, while snickering, Stephanie grabbed the hose, turned it on full blast, and handed it to my dad over the bushes. He stripped off his shorts behind the bushes and started spraying down his bottom and legs. For some reason, my sister and I were not phased as we looked around the neighborhood wondering if any of the neighbors were watching. My dad started laughing and said, "This is what I call a Honyak shower!" After a good rinsing he said to me in a low hush, "Chris, can you run in and get me some underwear, running shorts, and a plastic bag?" With my dad, what you see is what you get!

My dad was not perfect, he was human. Sometimes my dad was quick to anger. He could often be too blunt for his own good. And some of my siblings thought he played favorites, calling me his "golden child." I tried to tell them he wasn't playing favorites, he just liked having a son who daily brought him his slippers and newspaper, made him breakfast in bed with fried Spam, laughed at all his jokes, and helped him get farther in Super Mario 3 on the Nintendo. Well, that last sentence may be fudging the truth a bit, but he did love it when I could get Mario to defeat Bowser in the haunted castle. But as a frail human, there is one major hang-up that my dad could never get over; when it came to going to the doctor, he was more stubborn than a Middle Eastern donkey! He hated the doctor. "Don," my mom would say, "You need to make an appointment for a checkup. It has been over a few years since you had your heart looked at."

"Nah, I'm feeling just fine." He would say. "I'll just go walking with the dog and that will keep me fit."

One way he avoided the doctor was priding himself on being a naturalist. He believed if you found just the right kinds of herbs, vitamins, complete with a heavy application of Tiger Balm, you could fight any cold and virus. You can forget the local physician when you have a witch doctor for a father.

One of his favorite medicinal concoctions was a drink he made out of apple vinegar, molasses, honey, seltzer water, grapefruit juice, a mysterious brown liquid, salt, and some funny-looking plants he found in the back yard. He called the drink "Jog in a Jug." He told us if you drank one cup of the mysterious elixir, it was like you went running ten miles. The only time I took a drink of it, my throat started burning and my forehead was sweating streams of perspiration. "See," he said with delight, "don't you feel great, just like you ran a marathon?"

"No, Dad," I grimaced, "I feel like I just drank a cup of diesel fuel." I never touched "Jog in a Jug" again.

A DEEP AND DARK SEPTEMBER

The regular summer routine for my own family over the years was to spend a week with my wife's side of the family at Silver Lake Sand Dunes in Michigan, then later in the summer we would spend a week with my mom and dad at their home in Cleveland, Ohio. When we went to visit my parents in Cleveland they always made sure there was plenty to do: the pool was sparkling clean and ready for swimming, the candy jars of gummi bears and sour neon worms were stocked full, and of course, my mom always made her famous chili to greet us when we arrived. I love my mom's chili.

Well, when we came to visit in the summer of 2006 everything seemed to be as it always was. The kids were excited to hug their grandparents and the pool was open for business. Life was good and the visit for my family was better than expected that week, all except for one conversation I overheard between my mom and dad while I had my eyes closed resting on the back patio. My dad was in the nearby kitchen chewing on a small carrot talking about how tired he felt recently, and he mentioned that when he sat in the air conditioning at work it was making him shiver to his bones. Once again, my mom insisted that he go see the doctor, but being the stubborn man that he was, he brushed aside her concern and went out to play with our kids. During my time with my dad that week, he seemed a bit more worn down than normal but nothing that set off any alarm bells for me. I figured people get old and they slow down. Why should I think my dad would be any different?

We had a great week in Cleveland, and when we got back to Michigan our season for summer vacation was over; it was time to get ready for the back-to-school grindstone to begin. Life moves fast when you have four kids who are all in elementary school, so it's hard to think about much else. But after about two weeks into the normal routine of driving kids back and forth, I started to think about my dad and how he was acting during our visit. One early September morning after I just dropped off my kids, a strange thought came over me, "What if my dad died?" I wasn't prepared for it, but I couldn't get it out of my mind.

I instantly went back to a conversation I had with my mom when she told me about the time when my dad's father died. She said it shook my dad so badly it was years before he could step foot in a church building. She admitted to me that he dealt with a bit of residual anger concerning his dad's death and that some of the only words he uttered during that time was, "Oh how I loved that man." So it got me thinking, how would I respond if my dad died? Would I be mad? Would I have to take off a couple of months from preaching? Would I blame God? But then the thought went away and I went back to living life.

September 26, 2006, my phone rang, it was 2:00 a.m., and it was dark. As a pastor, I always hate receiving calls past 9:00 p.m. because you never know what crisis may be brewing on the other end of the line. "Chris, this is your mom." She sounded confused and desperate, I gulped some air and it felt like I swallowed my heart. "The paramedics just took your dad to the hospital…" Time stopped.

"I am not sure what is wrong with him, but it doesn't look good." I asked her what happened. "Your dad was resting on his recliner in the living room, and I was sleeping in the bedroom when I heard a gasping sound and ran into the living room where your dad sat with his eyes open. He wasn't breathing." My mom was breathing heavy as she said the words neither of us ever wished to utter or believe, "I hope they got here in time, but Chris, it just doesn't look good." My mom then said, "I gotta go. Please, my dear son, pray…" Then the phone hung up.

I don't know how to explain the next couple of hours, but a deep feeling of dark grief wrapped around my chest, sunk its sharp claws in me and it wouldn't let go. It was squeezing the very life out of me. I could do nothing but lie on the bed and sob. For the next hour, words would not come to me, but torrents of hot tears and guttural cries of anguish flowed freely. I knew my dad was either dead or dying, and I was more than sure it was a massive heart attack that killed him. That was why he was so tired that summer, and that is why he shivered in the air conditioning. Damn my dad's stubbornness! I told my wife to pray and she hugged me through the acute pain. Finally, I got a call from my mom again an hour later, it was confirmed, my dearest dad died.

I didn't want to believe it. But it was true. My dad died.

SIMPLY, "THANK YOU!"

My dad was my best friend. And the cruelty of death is that it doesn't let you have time to share last words or catch your breath and consider what happened. I needed to pack the kids and head to Cleveland for his funeral. The next day I talked to my mom, my sisters, and my brother and we were all planning to get to Cleveland to make arrangements together the next day to plan for the service and burial. I had one day to get my family and myself ready. My wonderful wife knew I was losing it, so she pulled me aside and said, "Chris, take this day off for yourself. I will make sure all the packing is done and the kids are ready to travel tomorrow. You need some time alone."

So I went into the backyard of our house and made a bonfire to process my thoughts and feelings. As the fire burned my mind drifted as I watched the flames, my mouth was saying nothing. For the next two to three hours, wonderful memories of my dad started saturating my mind. The endless hours we threw the football together in the backyard, my sisters laughing at some silly joke he told, I remembered his giant shoulders as I got a piggy-back ride from him as he slowly waded into the Atlantic Ocean because he knew I was scared of sharks, his jet-black Elvis hair, and most of all his smile and laugh. I loved his laugh. And then my thoughts drifted towards God. Was I going to be mad at him? Was I going to yell at the top of my lungs saying his death was unfair? Was I going to abandon the faith because the pain of losing your best friend is too much to see any goodness in the world?

No, none of that happened. All I could do is say, "Thank you, God! Thank you for having Don Weeks be my dad! Thank you for the incredible memories I have until the day I die. And thank you for giving me a person who taught me how to be a man." That is all I said. That is all I could say. I continued sitting by the fire for another hour wiping unrelenting tears of gratitude from my face. I realized more than anything at that moment that the grace of God has been showered upon me for 40 years living under the leadership of a man who really knew God. I also knew that anger at such a sublime moment like this would be a sin.

The next day our whole family gathered at my mom's house, our purpose was to plan, and more importantly, to sit together and remember. Each car that pulled up to the driveway carried a person that loved this man. Tears upon tears dropped every time a car door opened and a familiar face appeared. Warm hugs and embraces were exchanged. Laughter at the strangest times erupted. That whole day was a mysterious and loving mess. Later in the evening, my brother Don asked if he could talk to me alone. "Sure," I said.

"Chris," he gently instructed me as only an older brother could, "I think you should be the one who does Dad's eulogy. I know everyone would agree with me." I looked at him bewildered, "Don, are you sure? I'm not sure I can do it. I'm not sure I want to do it."

"Chris, you have to do it." He was right. So I sat down to write.

A FUNERAL FOR MY BEST FRIEND

A few days later a memorial service was given for my dad, Donald Charles Weeks. It was both a celebration of my dad's life and a worship service to our Father God who gave each of us life. Together, as a united family, we sang "In Christ Alone". especially belting out the last stanza:

> *No guilt in life, no fear in death,*
> *This is the power of Christ in me*
> *From life's first cry to final breath,*
> *Jesus commands my destiny*
> *No power of hell, no scheme of man,*
> *Can ever pluck me from His hand*
> *Till He returns or calls me home*
> *Here in the power of Christ I'll stand*

What an incredible promise. Jesus commands my dad's destiny: Don Weeks was created by God, sustained by God, and welcomed home by God. As a pastor you will see that over time you will participate in some "bad" funerals and some "good" funerals; well, my dad's was a "great" funeral. All of his children knew what he believed, and what my dad believed he also lived.

During the eulogy, I was able to share my heart about my love for my dad and then two testimonies from my sisters Gina and Stephanie were given. At some funerals it is like pulling teeth to get people to share memories, but at my dad's it was hard to limit our words on what we wanted to share about him. When it was all said and done, God was honored, people were blessed, and my mom was happy.

And then it hit me, standing next to my mom and watching her face as people offered her condolences concerning the great memories left by my dad, she was whole and free because she carried no shame. This is the greatest gift a man can give his wife, and a dad can give his children: Don Weeks left this earth with no baggage! No skeletons were hiding in a secret closet and nothing embarrassing spilled out that my mom had to give an account for before her friends and family. She truly was loved by my dad till death. I could see it on her face.

Later at the graveside my mom and brother Don were driving in the front of the procession right behind the hearse that was carrying my dad. My mom noticed the license plate read, "44"—it was my dad's football number he wore in college. She pointed it out to Don and he replied, "This is the best run of his life!"

One of the scariest verses in the whole of the Bible is found in the book of Ecclesiastes 5:4-7. It reads,

"When you make a vow to God, do not delay to fulfill it. He has no pleasure in fools; fulfill your vow. It is better not to make a vow than to make one and not fulfill it. Do not let your mouth lead you into sin. And do not protest to the temple messenger, "My vow was a mistake." Why should God be angry at what you say and destroy the work of your hands?"

When a man stands up before a congregation and says "I do" to the woman that he loves, he is making a vow. And it is the most important vow he will make his whole life. Not only are the people in the church there to witness this promise of love, but God is also watching! And as Ecclesiastes warns, "Fulfill your vow, because our holy God has no pleasure in fools!" I am proud to say that my dad was no fool—he died being faithful to the greatest promise a man can give—to cherish his wife until death.

LOVE COVERS

No one is perfect. Even in the best of times, a dad is bound to make mistakes, say words that hurt, will stay too long at work disappointing a child waiting at home to throw a baseball. These sorts of mistakes over time can be healed and forgotten because scripture says, "Love covers a multitude of sins." But a dad who breaks his vow and leaves his wife, cheats on her, or treats her only as a second-hand maid, rips a tear in the fabric of a family that is next to impossible to mend. Unfaithfulness is causing children not to trust their fathers, nor do their sons want to someday be fathers. Their daughter learns that men cannot be trusted, and as a result, it is why women these days are doing everything they can to protect themselves and prove they can go it just fine in the cold world on their own. This is one of the prime reasons dads no longer seem to matter.

Breaking a vow of marriage is dangerous because it warps the definition of love. Ephesians 5:31-32, *"For this reason a man will leave his father and mother and be united to his wife, and the two will become one flesh." This is a profound mystery – but I am talking about Christ and the church."* Marriage reflects the image of God to the world, and displaying his love is a major part of it. God's love is to be unconditional, nothing is supposed to stop it, love is said to always hope.

And of course, true love never fails.

So I am proud to say, my dad loved my mom, and by loving my mom he loved me, my brother, and my four sisters. And now that he is in heaven, I am sure Jesus himself has rewarded him for keeping his word. My dad may be gone, but his wonderful memory will live on.

CONCLUSION:
Seeing His Face

"Blessed are the pure in heart;
for they shall see God."
— *Matthew 5:8*

As I was nearing the end of writing this book, I was in the middle of a Sunday preaching series at my church concerning "The Sermon on the Mount." This series of proclamations found in the gospel of Matthew is considered Jesus' Magnum Opus, for it contains the secret keys that allow entrance for a person into the glorious Kingdom of God. Jesus tells us how we can have a blessed life, a happy existence starting now and lasting until eternity. Nearing the end of his discussion on the "beatitudes" Jesus says that those who are pure in heart will see God. Let that sink in a second. Believers will get to see the Holy and perfect one that no one earth could ever see before. If they did, they would die. Jesus presents this sublime promise as the fulfillment of all of our dreams, the pot at the end of the rainbow for the seeker of God.

But compared to salvation, having a new body, walking the golden streets, why will "seeing his face" be so great? As I was meditating on this question, another story about my dad flashed vividly in my mind. I want to share it as a final salvo to his memory.

BLIZZARD

I had a next-door neighbor named Scott. He was a kind little boy who at the age of seven lost his dad. On a dark and snowy night, his father was coming home from work and a sudden blizzard appeared, making travel extremely dangerous. About five miles from his house, the car his dad was driving hit a patch of black ice which caused him to spin out of control, slide down a ditch and smash into a tree. Scott's dad died on impact. It was tragic. In the blink of an eye, Scott lost a dad, and his mom lost a husband.

I can remember hearing the news. My mom and dad sat me down in the living room of our house and told me what happened and then they asked me to do my best to be a friend to Scott. Over the next few years, I was asked to babysit for him a number of times so his mom could pick up some extra money on her night shift job to make ends meet. I would walk over to Scott's house after dinner and wait until midnight for his mom to come home. It was a very strange time and it heightened my anxiety anytime a snowstorm was forecasted on television. I instantly grew paranoid when I saw the scrolling bar on the bottom of the screen issuing a Winter Storm Warning. And when that first fat snowflake would fall from the sky my heart would begin to sink.

To make matters worse, my own father traveled an awful lot for his work. Every week he would fly out of Cleveland on Sunday night and fly back home the following Thursday night after a very busy work schedule. If it was snowing outside on his return trip I would always be a bit nervous about his drive home, wondering if he too would meet the same fate as Scott's dad.

One Thursday night in December, my dad was scheduled to arrive at Cleveland Hopkins Airport late in the evening. The forecast was not good; possible heavy wet snow with 25 mph winds. It was forecasted as a warning, but over time it could turn into a possible blizzard. My mom called the airport to make sure the plane was arriving, and everything was still on schedule. When my dad's plane touched down, he called us up on the phone from the airport lobby telling us he was waiting for his luggage and would be on his way. "See you soon," he said to my mom.

"Be careful and take your time." My mom replied. After she hung up the phone she went to the kitchen to read a book, grabbed a cup of Maxwell House coffee, and began to eat a pomegranate. My mom was always as cool as a cucumber, trusting my dad's driving skills implicitly. But not me, I was always expecting the worst. My heart began to race as images of black ice, car crashes, cracked windshields, bent tire frames, and blood paraded across my fevered mind. I couldn't stop the worry spigot in my brain from flowing.

On a normal day, it took my dad approximately twenty to thirty minutes to make it home from the airport. So I started watching the clock. Fifteen minutes went by, then twenty minutes, and then thirty. No sign of my dad. I went to the front living room to look out the window and all I saw was horizontal snow—and it was piling up on the ground really fast. "Mom, do you think dad will be alright?" I said anxiously.

"Yes Chris, your dad is a great driver. Go watch television or play pool downstairs. He will be just fine." My mom said as she took another slow sip of coffee, still engrossed in her book.

I went to the front room and positioned myself on the chair near the window so I could keep my eye on the road, waiting for a flash of headlights. Nothing. Forty-five minutes went by, still nothing. Then a whole hour passed and with no sign whatsoever of my dad. I was losing my mind. "Mom, where is he?" My mom didn't hear because I could tell she was on a good part in her book.

I began to pace the floor imaging everything that could go wrong. It was a good hour and a half and by this time I was a basket-case. I think I grew ten years older from worry waiting in the front room for my dad. Seconds were like hours, minutes were years. It felt like my spider-sense was on high gear and all of life was in slow motion as worry began to squeeze tight in my chest.

But wait, I saw something. Yes, two dim little lights appeared at the very end of the street and they started heading up the road toward our house. It was slow going, but sure enough, they were getting closer. As the lights got brighter and brighter, worry's chokehold on my heart started to loosen. And then it was confirmed, it was my dad's car—a silver Chrysler Cordoba with a white leather top, pulled into our driveway. The snow was deep, but the car tires plowed a path through.

By this time my nose was pressed against the window and it was steaming it up, but I didn't care, I wanted to see my dad. The driver's side door opened and then I saw him! He could see the light shining from the house window and he knew it was me. Smiling, he gave me a salute that meant, "I made it and I am alright." My dad was home and seeing his face was enough.

And now as I write this, even though he is gone from this earth, I know I will get to see his face again. Jesus promised it. In the book of John, he said those who believe in him will live, even though they die. My dad believed and because he trusted in Jesus' words, I know he is alive. He is simply on the other side waiting, and someday I am going to see his face again. And not only his, but I will see the face of God! C. S. Lewis has a quote that expresses the beauty of the Christian hope of eternity:

"We are very shy nowadays of even mentioning heaven. We are afraid of the jeer about 'pie in the sky', and of being told that we are trying to 'escape' from the duty of making a happy world here and now into dreams of a happy world elsewhere. But either there is 'pie in the sky' or there is not. If there is not, then Christianity is false, for this doctrine is woven into its whole fabric. If there is, then this truth, like any other, must be faced, whether it is useful at political meetings or no. Again, we are afraid that heaven is a bribe, and that if we make it our goal we shall no longer be disinterested. It is not so. Heaven offers

nothing that a mercenary soul can desire. It is safe to tell the pure in heart that they shall see God, for only the pure in heart want to."

There is pie in the sky, and my dad is eating it. It is probably lemon meringue, his favorite. If there was no heaven, the person of Donald Charles Weeks would be nothing more than a sweet dream which lasted a little while and has now faded away forever. The longer someone you love has been gone, the more their memory is forgotten. Without the hope of heaven, life would be nothing more than a sick joke making a mockery of the loss of my best friend. But if heaven is real, then not only is he alive, but I will get to see him again! I will hear his laughter, see his smile, and maybe sweat up in some heavenly car garage attic while my mom says, "What are you two Honyaks doing up there?"

And I will get to see Jesus. The one who made my dad, the one who made me. And if he knew how to make the perfect dad just for me, just think what his heaven will be like for all those who believe?

Everything we ever hoped for or imagined.

CHASING SHEEP

8 VITAL TOPICS FOR THOSE CONSIDERING PASTORAL MINISTRY

christopherjweeks

MY SILENT SISTER
and her RUSTY CAGE

CHRISTOPHER J. WEEKS

SHAPKA AND COFFEE

A COLLECTION OF NONCONFORMIST CONSERVATIVE CHRISTIAN RAMBLINGS

christopherjweeks

NEW BELIEVERS
A FOUR WEEK STUDY GUIDE

christopherjweeks

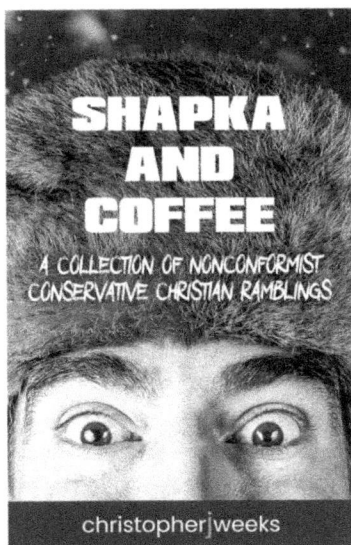

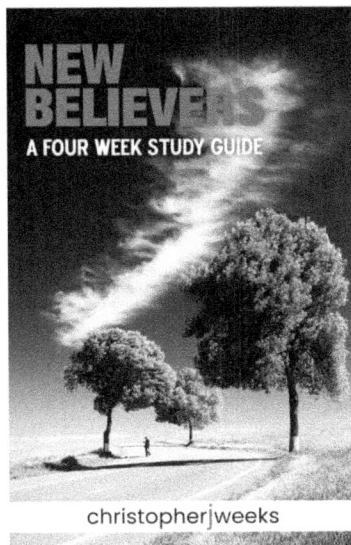

www.christopherjweeks.com

www.ingramcontent.com/pod-product-compliance
Lightning Source LLC
LaVergne TN
LVHW051230080426
835513LV00016B/1510